FAITH BASICS
THE SPIRIT–EMPOWERED LIFE

Beth Jones

D0905952

Unless otherwise noted, all Scripture quotations are taken from the New King James Version of the Bible. Copyright © 1979, 1980, 1982, Thomas Nelson, Inc., Publishers.

Scripture quotations marked The Message are taken from THE MESSAGE. Copyright ©1993, 1994, 1995, 1996, 2000, 2001, 2002 by Eugene H. Peterson. Used by permission of NavPress Publishing Group.

Scripture quotations marked NLT are taken from the *Holy Bible, New Living Translation*, copyright © 1996, 2004, 2007 by Tyndale House Foundation. Used by permission of Tyndale House Publishers, Inc., Carol Stream, Illinois 60188. All rights reserved.

All Scripture quotations marked NIV are taken from The Holy Bible: New International Version® NIV®. Copyright © 1973, 1978, 1984 by International Bible Society. Used by permission of Zondervan Publishing House. All rights reserved.

Scripture quotations marked AMP are taken from the Amplified® Bible, copyright © 2015 by The Lockman Foundation. Used by permission. (www.Lockman.org).

Scripture quotations marked AMPC are taken from the Amplified® Bible, copyright © 1954, 1958, 1962, 1964, 1965, 1987 by The Lockman Foundation. Used by permission. (www.Lockman.org).

Scripture quotations marked ERV are taken from the HOLY BIBLE: EASY-TO-READ VERSION © 2001 by World Bible Translation Center, Inc. and used by permission.

20 19 18 17 16   10 9 8 7 6 5 4 3 2 1

Faith Basics
The Spirit—Empowered Life: Find Your Flow
Copyright © 2016 Beth Jones
www.jeffandbethjones.org

ISBN: 978-168031-058-0

Published by Harrison House Publishers
Tulsa, OK 74145
www.harrisonhouse.com

Printed in the United States of America
All rights reserved under International Copyright Law. Contents and/or cover may not be reproduced in whole or in part without the expressed written consent of the Publisher.

CONTENTS

INTRODUCTION

———◆———

You know that feeling when you have a big secret and you can't wait to share it with your friends? Or when you've been keeping a surprise party hush–hush for months and the time finally arrives for you to pop out from behind a couch and yell, "Surprise!!!" That's how I feel about sharing this book with you, dear reader! I want to huddle up with you so I can yell, "Surprise!" as we dig in to the basics of God's Word and explore this thing called the Spirit–empowered life.

I picture you as I write.

I see you, young people who care about making a difference, and you're hungry for all God has for you. I see you, new Christians taking things one step at a time. I see you, authentic believers who sincerely desire the power of the Spirit so you can reach your family and friends for Jesus. I see lots of you who have grown up in church but got bored, disinterested or tired of going through the motions, so you faded. You didn't know the Lord had so much more for you. I see many of you, who don't know what you don't know about the Spirit–empowered life, and in some cases, you've been told to stay away from "those people"— so you hold on to a lifeless tradition or an accepted form of godliness, while your heart thirsts for more.

Others of you are well versed in the Spirit–empowered life and have been enjoying your relationship with the Lord and being full of His Spirit for years. You pastor churches, lead gospel outreach ministries in communities, teach Bible studies, minister to young people, and help the less fortunate; and you are looking for a practical, hands-on teaching tool to guide those in your sphere of influence into the dynamic Spirit–empowered life. As I write, I am praying this book will help you help others.

No matter where you are in your journey, I am writing this book for you.

I'll bet good numbers of you are connected with me through the *Getting a Grip on the Basics* books or the *Life Basics Bible Studies*—we've been traveling these roads in God's Word together for many years, haven't we? You'll notice this book (and all the books coming in this new Faith Basics series) are a combination of the workbook style teaching you've grown accustomed to combined with a lot more stories and fun! I hope you enjoy this new era of books and you continue to *get a grip* on those basics!

If you are eager to get into this study to learn more about what God has for you (or what we call every pastor's dream), feel free to skip the rest of this introduction and get on over to the My Story section.

Others of you may need to move a little slower to see how the dots connect. I'm right there with you. A few decades ago, the dots started to connect for me, and I had a couple of surprise awakenings. I have a feeling you are on the threshold of an awakening, too!

You see, I discovered that I had a whole picnic basket full of bologna sandwiches (my ideas, thoughts, opinions, experiences and fears), and whenever I came upon a spiritual crossroads in my life, the Lord asked me to trust Him by trading a sandwich for His much better feast of goodness. In other words, sometimes I had to trade or "unlearn" some things before I could receive or learn the new things He wanted for me.

You also may be full of baloney—drats, I mean bologna— holding on tight to your own ideas, thoughts, opinions, experiences, and fears, and perhaps it's tasting a bit stale. Like me, you may have to "unlearn" some things in order to learn the new things He wants to teach you. If you think God might have more in store and you're open to the idea of trading your bologna sandwich for the Spirit– empowered life, read on.

Remember, whenever God asks for something from us, it's because He's trying to get something better—like an awakening—to us. (Try to remember that little nugget; it will really help you on the road to the Spirit–empowered life.)

As you go through the book, you will notice an ebb and flow. One minute I'll be sharing stories with you and the next minute we'll be straight into teaching mode looking up numerous Scriptures, filling in blanks, and listening to what the Spirit wants us to know. I am all about helping you get the basics and enjoying the process, so we'll keep it personal, encouraging, and motivating, and then *boom*! We'll teach, teach, teach!

I believe at the end, you'll have something tangible in God. You'll experience something that will forever change your life. The Spirit– empowered life won't just be the greatest sounding theory, it will be your reality. And just so we're on the same page, when I say "Spirit– empowered," I'm talking about the whole enchilada, first being born of the Spirit then filled with the Spirit—which conveniently is what this book is all about.

In our four sessions, we will cover these basics:

Getting to Know the Holy Spirit

Being Filled with the Holy Spirit

Praying in the Holy Spirit

Being Led by the Holy Spirit.

To get you on your way, let me encourage you with three quick instructions.

1. PRAY SOMETHING LIKE THIS

"Father, I ask You to open my eyes to all You want to do in me and through me. I pray for the spirit of wisdom and understanding as I learn what it means to live the Spirit–empowered life. I want everything You desire for me, and I don't want anything You don't want for me. Thank You in advance for all that You are about to do in me. In Jesus' Name. Amen."

2. START AS SOON AS NOW

Don't put this book in the "I should do this someday pile." Make a decision to get started now. All you need is an open heart, your Bible, and a pen *(because there are lots of blanks to fill in).*

3. TURN ON YOUR EXPECTATION

Fasten your seatbelt. Expect God to take you on a wonderful ride in His Word and into a greater experience of knowing and flowing with the Holy Spirit.

Okay friends, are you ready? Here we go.

START HERE: MY STORY

—◆—

I want to start by sharing my story with you. While we all have our own unique stories, sometimes hearing about someone else's journey helps us to relax and open up our heart to all that the Lord has in store for us. I hope you resonate and connect with various parts of my experience and are encouraged as you run full on into the Spirit–empowered life!

BEING BORN OF THE SPIRIT

I remember the first time I noticed Spirit–empowered Christians. I was not yet a committed follower of Christ but during my freshman year in college, I watched Andi, my roommate (whom I had been friends with since third grade), live a life that was full of love for others and with a contented joy. During our senior year of high school, she had become a born–again Christian. It was attractive. Now as her room-mate, I watched her get up early in the morning to read her Bible, and peace seemed to ooze out of her.

Meanwhile, my life was quite different. Although I had been raised as a Catholic, I was not living for the Lord. Whatever my roommate had, I did not. Acting like I was happy, smoking my cigarettes and living the party life was the way to a good time, in my book. At least that's what I told myself. Deep down, I was empty. I had felt empty for some time but had never taken time to recognize it or admit it. Maybe it was because I felt so capable of running my own life, that I couldn't accept or didn't want to know my role as "lord of my life" wasn't working.

I was ten years old when my dad left, and I distinctly remember taking on the "lordship" of my own life and the responsibility of growing up overnight to help my mom. I was in third grade when I called my three younger sisters together for a meeting in the basement. I gave them the plan: "Ok you guys, since we now come from a broken home, everyone is going to expect us to drop out of school and start doing drugs. But we aren't going to do that. We're going to stay out of trouble, get good grades, and be good kids." I didn't ask for any questions or feedback. This was just what we were going to do. The Big Sister of Oz had spoken! Turns out we were good kids; we did stay out of trouble and got good grades—and we partied just enough without getting caught. (When I say we were good kids, I mean good enough. I probably shouldn't have introduced them to the art of stealing cigarettes from Mom's purse or taught them how to keep the vodka liquid level in Mom's stash by replacing what we borrowed with water. Ok, so I wasn't the *perfect* big sister.)

Watching my childhood friend and roommate float around our dorm room with this radiant love, joy, and peace forced me to come face-to-face with my own internal emptiness, and I had to admit that my best efforts at lordship were not enough. I definitely did not have what she had.

To top off all of my internal emptiness and to convince me thoroughly of my need for a Savior, the Lord must have made certain we were assigned to share our dorm suite with two other suitemates who were super cool, super cute, super rich, and had super good-looking boyfriends. For someone who was not easily intimidated, I started to feel insecure for the first time in my life. Kim and Kimmie (yes, their actual names) had everything a girl could want—plus they had beautiful, long straight hair. I had short, thick, wavy hair, and the waves were not in the right places. When I upgraded my hairstyle to a permed mullet, it didn't help. They had nice, expensive clothes, and I had an eclectic mix of thrift store tomboy jeans, Converse tennis shoes, and turtlenecks. They had earrings and bracelets made of real gold, and I had cheap costume jewelry I took from my mom's jewelry box. And their homes? Can't even go there. Massive. They were the size of apartment buildings that could house 56 people. We lived in a small duplex. My bedroom was in the basement, and my walls were covered in red shag carpet, literally.

Compared to my angelic roommate and my super perfect suitemates, the emptiness I felt inside enlarged. After several conversations with Andi and visiting a Bible Study with her (only to see if there were any cute boys—totally wrong motives, I know), I started to read the Bible in secret. And, to my surprise, God was in His Bible. Seriously. He was in it. It was alive, and I felt like He was sitting on my shoulder speaking to my heart whenever I cracked open the pages. I seemed to know that Jesus was knocking on the door of my heart, asking me to open up and give Him my heart—or rather allow Him to come into my heart. Of course, I argued, debated, pondered, and delayed making any decisions about the Lord. I only opened the door a crack to talk to Him for a few minutes, but I kept the chain lock engaged, never inviting Him in. What I was holding onto, I don't know. He was patient.

By the end of my freshman year, I was ready to open the door fully and invite Jesus in. The change came as I was reading the Bible.

I simply realized the truth. I was a sinner (a good person, but a sinner nonetheless), and I needed a Savior. Jesus was that loving Savior. So in May of 1978, sitting at a friend's kitchen table, I received Jesus into my life and declared Him as my Lord. When I blurted out, "Ok you guys, I'm gonna be a Christian," that was it. That was the extent of my salvation prayer. *Poof,* just like that, I was born of the Spirit and became a born–again Christian.

My permed mullet remained intact, and my fake gold earrings didn't turn to 14 karat gold, but I did experience God's complete forgiveness and an internal satisfaction like I had never known. I felt new joy in this relationship with the Lord and I couldn't get over this book—the Bible! The Bible was unlike any of the textbooks I was reading. It was alive, and God was speaking to my heart daily. I felt the flow of His peace fill the deepest part of me and for the first time in my life, I experienced the reality of never being alone. It was wonderful! I recall literally thinking that the sky was bluer and the birds were chirping more sweetly than I ever remembered.

Knowing Jesus radically changed my life from the inside and eventually, the outside.

Perhaps you're like I was, living your life, empty inside and knowing you need Jesus. Maybe you realize, like I did, that you are a sinner and you need a Savior. The Bible says, "If you openly declare that Jesus is Lord and believe in your heart that God raised him from the dead, you will be saved. For it is by believing in your heart that you are made right with God, and it is by openly declaring your faith that you are saved" (Romans 10:9-10, NLT.) If you've never surrendered and personally invited Jesus to be the Lord of your life but you'd like to, let's start our study by giving you the opportunity to be born again.

You could say what I said to the Lord, in front of your family or friends, "Ok you guys, I'm gonna be a Christian." When I did it, it was from my heart. I meant it, and it stuck.

If you want a more "official" prayer, you could go with this one:

Father, I want to be born again. Dear Lord Jesus, I know I am a sinner, and I need Your forgiveness. I believe in my heart that You died for my sins and rose from the dead. Today, I confess with my mouth that You are my Lord. Thank You for forgiving my sins and causing me to be born of Your Spirit. From this day forward, I will follow You as my Lord and Savior. Guide my life and help me to do Your will. In Jesus' Name. Amen.

Congratulations! You're a born–again Christian!

BEING FILLED WITH THE SPIRIT

I loved this new life of being a Christian and getting to know Jesus on a daily basis. God's Word was so alive. The Lord seemed to customize my quiet times with Him as I journaled my prayers and everything I was learning and experiencing. Seriously, for the first three years of my Christian life, I was soaring high with the Lord, internally!

Meanwile, He was working a serious overhaul on my exterior—my habits, lifestyle and choices. The closer I got to the Lord, the more I desired to eliminate things that were contrary to Him.

I remember having to make some tough choices like walking away from a few ungodly influences who were trying to pull me in the wrong direction, getting rid of my trashy novels and most of my music albums and 8-tracks. (Obviously, this was before the Internet, iTunes, and digital downloads. Who am I kidding? This was before the invention of the home computer, CDs, and DVDs, around the time the last tyrannosaurus rex faded from earth.) One day as I read Acts 19, I began to have a desire to get rid of paraphernalia that didn't honor the Lord—so, I grabbed my stack of secular albums and flung them like Frisbees into a dumpster. (This was a true test of my faith as that music stash was probably half of my net worth. Thankfully, I was able to spare my Carpenters album and a Barry Manilow 8-track tape.)

While the Lord was working on my exterior habits, He patiently and simultaneously worked on sanctifying (cleaning up) my inner desires and habits including my language, my love affair with cigarettes and alcohol, my pride, fears, and judgmental attitudes, and my, shall we say, over-the-top sarcasm. (My apologies to the angels assigned to my case.)

What a season it was. I was growing. I loved Jesus, loved reading His Word and I loved getting to know Him better. When I got involved with a campus ministry, I learned how to share my faith and even led a few people to the Lord including most of my family. I was as "on fire" for the Lord as I knew to be, yet I noticed a few Christians who seemed to have a different type of joy and freedom in their relationship with the Lord—different than what I had—and I got thirsty for more.

The only problem? I heard they were *charismatics*, and I had been told by well-meaning mentors and friends that I should steer clear of—well, actually run from—those weird, emotional charismatic Christians who believed in being filled with the Spirit and speaking in tongues.

The fear of ending up like a spiritual weirdo, a trance-like zombie, or crazy Aunt Matilda who lives alone and talks in tongues to her sixteen cats, successfully kept me away from those charismatics. That is until Andi, my old college roommate, was filled with the Spirit and began to speak in tongues! I couldn't believe it! She wasn't weird. She wasn't emotional. She was normal, *and* she was the one who had led me to the Lord! In her, I saw the fruit of the Holy Spirit in love, joy, and peace; but I also saw the power of the Spirit flowing in her life—she had boldness I desired. She had been filled with the Spirit and her ability to talk about Jesus with others and her freedom to worship the Lord was attractive to me.

Andi explained to me what being "filled with the Spirit" was all about, but because I had been taught to stay away from "those people" and from "speaking in tongues," I had to *unlearn* some things in order to actually learn new things. I was thirsty for all the Lord had for me and I really wanted to learn the truth, so I read all the books I could find on the subject of being filled with the Spirit and speaking in tongues. To be honest, the authors each had different opinions and all of the reading confused me! I decided to set all of the books aside, and I picked up my Bible and prayed, "Father, I am not a Bible scholar, but You know my heart, and I desire the truth. I want everything You want for me, and I don't want anything You don't want for me. As I read the Bible, please show me the truth. In Jesus' Name. Amen."

I began to read the Books of Acts and 1 Corinthians and other books in the Bible that contained passages about the Holy Spirit. After weeks of reading, I came to the conclusion that there *was* indeed such a thing as being filled with the Holy Spirit (also called being baptized with the Spirit or receiving the Spirit), which happens subsequent to being born again of the Spirit. I also came to the conclusion that I had not yet received this infilling of the Spirit, mainly because I didn't know how to get it! Until one night . . .

One Thursday night, Michelle, a Christian friend of mine, and I decided to visit a Bible study in town. We knew several of the people there. At this Bible study, the man in charge welcomed us to the group and asked us to share our personal testimonies. I shared my salvation testimony with the group and then Michelle did the same. When we finished, the man asked us, "So, when were you girls filled with the Spirit?" My eyes grew wide, and I said, "Uh, well that's the thing. I have been reading about this experience and I don't think I have been filled with the Spirit. I don't how to receive it." My friend Michelle said the same thing. The man smiled as if to say, "You girls have come to the right place!"

At the end of the Bible study, he asked Michelle and me if we wanted to be filled with the Spirit and we both said, yes! They put two chairs in the middle of the room, and he and his wife and the other college kids gathered around us, laid hands on our shoulders, and began to pray. Immediately, I heard people around us praying in foreign languages, which I took to be tongues. The man leading the Bible study asked me and Michelle to repeat a prayer after him, and we said something like, "Father, I am a born–again Christian, but tonight I ask You to fill me with Your Spirit. I am hungry for more of You and I receive the infilling of Your Spirit right now. In Jesus' Name. Amen."

When we said "Amen," I was excited because I believed I had received the very thing we had just asked for. I was ready to open my eyes and stand up from the circle when the man said, "Ok girls, just yield to the Spirit, and speak in tongues. Go ahead and speak in the words that are bubbling up from the river inside of you."

I remember thinking, *What river? I don't have any words to say, and I don't feel any river bubbling up inside me.* The group continued to lay hands on us and pray in tongues. I kept looking for a bubbling river, but I felt like a dried up creek! Then, like a terrible person, as I sat there in the middle of the circle, I prayed that they would stop praying!

I honestly didn't feel any type of river bubbling up and even if I did, I wasn't going to speak in tongues in front of everyone! Eventually the group stopped praying for us and removed their hands from our shoulders. I think they may have been disappointed that I didn't speak in tongues. But I left the Bible study that night on cloud nine (even with a dry creek!) certain that I had received the baptism of the Spirit.

Five days later, on a Tuesday, I was home kneeling by my bed, spending time in prayer when I said, "Lord, I want to praise You from my innermost being. I want to tell You so many things, but I just don't have words to tell You. I feel like I just keep repeating the same thing over and over, 'I love You Lord; I praise You Jesus,' but it seems like there are more words I want to say to worship You. I think if I could speak in those tongue words, I could praise You the way I want to."

I felt the Lord speak to my heart and say, "You're being too analytical and logical about this. Your mind keeps talking you out of it. Just take your head off and put it on the shelf, then worship Me from your heart."

So, in my mind's eye, I took my head off and put it on the shelf. Within moments, I saw this word flash by my heart: *kadesh*. So, I said it out loud, "*kadesh*." Then I said to myself, "What am I doing, making up words now? What in the world is *kadesh*?" So, I took my head off the shelf and put it back on my body and got up from my prayer time half disappointed and half excited. *What was that all about?* I wondered, *Was* kadesh *a tongues word, or did I just make it up?*

A few days later on Thursday (one week after the people had prayed for us at the Bible study), my friend Michelle and I were at the Detroit Metro Airport getting ready to catch a flight to Boston to see old college friends. Michelle asked me, "Has anything happened to you since those people prayed for us?" I told her about my experience in prayer on Tuesday and the word *kadesh*.

I asked her if anything had happened to her since the night people had prayed for us, and she said she had a similar experience on Tuesday. She was home praying and the Lord spoke to her heart and told her to throw her fears in the wastebasket and worship Him from her heart. She said, "So, I threw my fears in the wastebasket and started to worship and magnify the Lord in this language of tongues. It felt like twenty years of praises to the Lord came out as I worshipped the Lord in tongues. It was wonderful!" Her face was lit up like a Christmas tree, and I thought to myself, *Great! She gets an entire language, and I get* kadesh*!* Then I whispered, "Lord, I'll yield now!"

We were just about to board a United flight heading to Boston, and I could hardly wait to let the river that was *now* bubbling up inside of me out! Once on board, I waited for the jet to take off and get to our cruising altitude so the seatbelt sign would go off and I could get to the airplane's restroom to pray (I assumed in those *kadesh* tongues). As soon as I was able to move about, I went to the restroom at 30,000 feet and had a wonderful time standing in that little space worshiping the Lord in a gusher of tongues!

Over the next few weeks as I prayed in tongues in my quiet times with the Lord, I heard myself say a few words numerous times, and I saw how they were spelled. The three words were *kadesh, hodiah,* and *shem.* I didn't know Hebrew, but somehow they sounded like Hebrew to me. My Bible had a cyclopedic index in the front section so on a whim, I decided to see if these words were there. To my surprise, they were!

The word *kadesh* meant, "holy." The word *hodiah* meant, "splendor of Jehovah" and *shem* meant, "renown." I was stunned and extremely blessed to discover this. To find that I was praising the Lord in tongues by calling Him "holy, the splendor of Jehovah and renown" was a real confirmation that this language was indeed given to me by the Holy Spirit. (As a person who had been taught to be skeptical of this type of experience and with my analytical approach to the whole subject, the supernatural confirmation of my first three words in tongues as actual Hebrew words that magnified the Lord settled the issue for me.)

In addition to speaking in tongues, I also noticed a fresh boldness in my spirit. I felt a new confidence to be a witness for Jesus and felt empowered to talk about the Lord with others. I sensed a new freedom to worship Him from my heart of hearts. When I read God's Word, it was as if the brightness dial had been turned up, and I started to see the truth-dots connect like I had never seen before. It was as if I had crossed a threshold in my spiritual walk with the Lord. That was many years ago, but it seems like yesterday.

I was born again in 1978 and filled with the Spirit in 1981, and it was game on—the Spirit–empowered life! Do you know I have never regretted one second? Knowing the love of my Father, the grace of Jesus, and having a friendship with the Holy Spirit has only made every part of my life better. Every day with the Lord *is* sweeter than the day before—not to mention it's a really fun faith-filled adventure! And that's why I am so excited to share this book with you. I know He has wonderful things ahead for you too!

So, where are you in your journey? Interested? Intrigued? Curious? If you are born again and thirsty for more of the Spirit–empowered life—to know the Holy Spirit, to be filled with the Spirit, to pray in the Spirit, and to be led by the Spirit—then let's jump into Chapter 1, "Getting to Know the Holy Spirit" with both feet!

SESSION 1:
GETTING TO KNOW
THE HOLY SPIRIT

———◆———

Ok, so Jesus begins His ministry. He's around 30 years of age. Up until then, He had been known as the carpenter's son and a really smart 12-year old who could reason the Scriptures with all the experts. (And also the child Mary and Joseph lost for a few days, but I digress.)

The point is—Jesus lived His normal life (if that is possible), and then something significant happened when Jesus was about 30 years of age. The next thing we know, Jesus and His ministry are on the map and the whole world changes. What happened?

Matthew 3 happened.

Matthew 3:16-17

When He had been baptized, Jesus came up immediately from the water; and behold, the heavens were opened to Him, and He saw the Spirit of God descending like a dove and alighting upon Him. And suddenly a voice came from heaven, saying, "This is My beloved Son, in whom I am well pleased."

What made the difference? It was the Holy Spirit.

We know Jesus began His life on earth in a supernatural way, conceived by the Spirit and born of a virgin—the God-man. The Scriptures tell us He grew in wisdom and stature and in favor with God and men, and He was anointed with joy more than anyone else. He must have been such a winsome person to be around. The Bible tells us He had the Holy Spirit without measure, yet when the time arrived for Jesus to begin His public ministry, He needed the additional help and empowerment of the Spirit. When the Spirit came upon Him, the results were evident as we watch His life unfold before us in the gospels. Jesus ministered to people with joy, power, mercy, and compassion through His supernatural teaching, preaching, healing, and miracle-working ministry. Then at the proper time, He laid down His life on the cross to shed His spotless blood and pay the penalty our sin demanded. After three days, the Holy Spirit quickened His body and raised Him from death, and then Jesus ascended and was seated at the right hand of the Father. And do you know one of the first things Jesus did just ten days after His ascension? He sent the Holy Spirit to the earth for us!

If Jesus, the Son of God, required the empowerment of the Holy Spirit, I don't want to sound like Sister Obvious, but so do we—more so.

Can you see that? Knowing God and living a life empowered by the Holy Spirit is the most enjoyable and supernatural way to live this side of heaven! This is the life. It's the one you hoped existed. So, let's start with a fresh look at God and the role of God the Father, Jesus the Son and the Holy Spirit.

A. THREE IN ONE

Have you ever wondered about the various words we use for God?

We call Him God, Father, Jesus, Baby Jesus, the Word Made Flesh, Lord, Sweet Lord, Spirit of God, Holy Spirit, Holy Ghost, Jehovah, Yahweh, Adonai, Emmanuel, and the Almighty. It's no wonder people are sometimes confused. What do all of these words mean? When we use these words, whom are we talking about?

In the Bible, God has literally revealed Himself as the Godhead (or what some people refer to as the Trinity). The Godhead, or Trinity, is simply God revealing Himself in three Persons: God the Father, God the Son, and God the Holy Spirit—not three Gods, not three manifestations of God but quite literally, three Persons in One God.

Theologians debate over the finer points of the Godhead or Trinity, but for our purposes, let's stay with the basics. The Father is God, but He is not Jesus the Son or the Holy Spirit (Mark 13:32, John 16:12-16). Jesus the Son is God, but He is not the Spirit or the Father, (John 14:16, 28). The Spirit is God, but He is not Jesus the Son or the Father (Galatians 4:6, John 16:12-16). Got it?

Let's take a closer look at knowing the Godhead.

1. Genesis 1:26 KJV

And God said, "Let us make man in our image, after our likeness . . ."

When God used the words *us* and *our* in this verse, does that represent a plural or singular idea? _____

_____

Who do you think *us* is referring to? _____

_____

_____

When it refers to man being created "in our image and after our likeness," who do you think *our* is referring to? _____

_____

_____

In the very beginning, God revealed Himself as one Godhead consisting of three persons—the Father, the Son, and the Holy Spirit.

2. Deuteronomy 6:4

Hear, O Israel: The Lord our God, the Lord is one!

How is the Lord our God described? _____

_____

_____

One: Scholars and theologians have written volumes on this verse and the word *one.* We agree with those who see this as a reference to the Godhead—Father, Son, and Holy Spirit—being *one* and in complete unity, harmony and oneness.[1]

3. 1 John 5:7

For there are three that bear witness in heaven: the Father, the Word, and the Holy Spirit; and these three are one.

How many witnesses are there in heaven? _____

_____

_____

Who are these witnesses? _____

_____

_____

We know this is a reference to the Godhead: the Father, Jesus "the Word" made flesh (according to John 1:14), and the Holy Spirit.

We know that these _____ are _____.

One God. Three persons.

The famous and familiar hymn *Holy, Holy, Holy* written by Reginald Heber in 1826 is all about the Godhead—Father, Son and Holy Spirit. Here are a few stanzas.

Holy, holy, holy! Lord God Almighty!
Early in the morning our song shall rise to thee.
Holy, holy, holy! Merciful and mighty,
God in three persons, blessed Trinity!

Holy, holy, holy! All the saints adore thee,
casting down their golden crowns around the glassy sea;
cherubim and seraphim falling down before thee,
which wert, and art, and evermore shalt be.

Holy, holy, holy! Though the darkness hide thee,
though the eye of sinful man thy glory may not see,
only thou art holy; there is none beside thee,
perfect in power, in love and purity.

Holy, holy, holy! Lord God Almighty!
All thy works shall praise thy name, in earth and sky and sea.
Holy, holy, holy! Merciful and mighty,
God in three persons, blessed Trinity

What does that mean to you and me? It means that we get to know the multi-faceted, rich dimensions of our one God (the Godhead) by getting to know the three Persons of the Godhead: the person of God the Father, the person of Jesus our Lord, and the person of the Holy Spirit.

B. KNOWING GOD THE FATHER

The Father wants you to know Him in a very real and personal way. He wants to talk to you, and He wants you to talk to Him. When you meet new friends, it takes many hours of communicating to really get to know them. The same is true in our relationship with the Lord. Yes, we are friends of God, but it goes deeper than that. We are His children. Let's look at it.

1. 1 John 4:8

. . . God is love.

What is God? _____

_____

He doesn't just have love; He is love. That is His nature, quite different from the bad rap He gets as a buzzkill Judge. God is love.

2. 1 John 3:1

Behold what manner of love the Father has bestowed on us, that we should be called children of God! . . .

What does this verse tell us about the Father? _____

_____

_____

What does this verse tell us about ourselves? _____

_____

_____

_____

I'll never forget the season in my life when I began to grasp God as my first and ultimate Father in a fresh new way. (My dear reader, I hope you can connect with what I am about to share, especially if you have struggled with what we sometimes call "the dad thing." If you've felt fatherless, orphaned, had a rocky or non-existent relationship with your earthly father, I believe this will help you.)

As a young girl and then as a teenager, my relationship with my earthly father was a bit of a roller coaster, and I always felt an undercurrent of rejection, disapproval, and disinterest from him. I don't think he intended for me to feel that way, but that is what often happens when a dad leaves his wife and young kids and is not around day to day. It's not that I didn't like visiting him at his trailer every other weekend—eating chips and dip and watching war movies was great and all (and probably would have been super great if me and my three sisters had been boys). I really believe my dad did the best job he could—especially with four daughters! I don't hold anything against him, he was actually quite charming and funny, and he taught all of us how to fish, put a worm on a hook and swing a golf club. Now that he is with the Lord, I have many fond memories of him and I look forward to an eternal reunion. Still, there was a huge "father gap" in my life.

(So, here's a quick shout out to all you dads. You have such a seriously important role. More than you know. I pray the Lord helps you to see how significant you are and I pray that you get so filled with the Father's love that you overflow and saturate your kids with love!)

Before we go further, here's something we need to talk about. If there is any epidemic we've seen over the years in ministry, it's this one: fatherless people. Girls without dads. Boys without fathers. Orphans running everywhere. The father gap is real for thousands upon thousands of people. Many of you feel just like I did—rejected, disapproved and unimportant. Maybe you lost your father or were abandoned, neglected, abused, or ignored. I am so sorry for you. It wasn't fair and it hurts—emotionally and sometimes physically. You missed out. You didn't get the love, support, a shoulder or the loving arms you deserved from a dad. I am really sorry for you. Sometimes, you just need to know that it's okay to grieve the loss of what you didn't get to experience in a father-child relationship. If that were the end of the story it would be just, sad. But it's not the end of the story. Our Heavenly Father wants to weigh in with the final chapter for you. He wants to fill the father gap as your true Father. I know it's true. I hope you will open your heart and allow Him to reveal Himself to you afresh.

So, this father gap had skewed my view of my Heavenly Father, until He began to reveal Himself to me as my first and ultimate Father in a fresh new way. He connected the dots for me between these two Scriptures: "**God is Spirit,** and those who worship Him must worship in spirit and truth" (John 4:24, emphasis mine), and "Furthermore, we have had human fathers who corrected us, and we paid them respect. Shall we not much more readily be in subjection to the **Father of spirits** and live?" (Hebrews 12:9, emphasis mine).

It hit me.

God is a Spirit. I am a spirit (and I have a soul and live in a body, but at my core, the real me is a spirit being). He is the Father of spirits! He is the Father of the real me!

I realized He used my mother and father to bring me into this world, but the real me is a spirit being and He, God who is the Father of spirits, is my real Father. Truly, He is the Father of me . . . and you! I don't know how that hits you, but it hit me like a ton of loved, accepted, approved, and interested bricks! The more Scriptures I read about my Father, the more I got to know Him, and the more loved, accepted and approved I felt! He wants this for you, too!

Then to make it even more personal and tangible, Jesus said, "He who has seen me has seen the Father" (John 14:9). He just took everything about knowing the Father to a level we can grasp. Jesus is the visible image of the invisible God. When we see Jesus in action, we get a real up close and personal view of what our Father is like!

Ok, let me give you the bottom line: God is the Father of you! Isn't that wonderful? Go ahead and shout or cry or something. Let's study on.

3. Ephesians 3:14-20 AMP

For this reason [grasping the greatness of this plan by which Jews and Gentiles are joined together in Christ] I bow my knees [in reverence] before the Father [of our Lord Jesus Christ], from whom every family in heaven and on earth derives its name [God—the first and ultimate Father]. May He grant you out of the riches of His glory, to be strengthened and spiritually energized with power through His Spirit in your inner self, [indwelling your innermost being and personality], so that Christ may dwell in your hearts through your faith. And may you, having been [deeply] rooted and [securely] grounded in love, be fully capable of comprehending with all the saints (God's people) the width and length and height and depth of His love [fully experiencing that amazing, endless love]; and [that you may come] to know [practically, through personal experience] the love of Christ which far surpasses [mere] knowledge [without experience], that you may be filled up [throughout your being] to all the fullness of God [so that you may have the richest experience of God's presence in your lives, completely filled and flooded with God Himself]. Now to Him who is able to [carry out His purpose and] do superabundantly more than all that we dare ask or think [infinitely beyond our greatest prayers, hopes, or dreams], according to His power that is at work within us, to Him be the glory in the church and in Christ Jesus throughout all generations forever and ever. Amen.

I don't think we realize how much our Father loves us. I know it's taken me all of my Christian life to barely get it. And just when I am oohing and ahhhing about how good God is, He's like, "You think that's the extent of My love? Here, did you know this?" and then He pulls out another one of His love buckets I didn't even know existed! The more He reveals about His goodness, mercy, and love, the more I wonder if I've ever really known it. The truth is, our Father loves us so much it will probably take eternity to plumb the depths, the height, width, and length of it! Still, He gives us this passage in Ephesians because as much as is possible in this life, He wants us to know for ourselves through experience His great love.

What do we learn about the Father's love in this passage? _____

_____

_____

_____

How does verse 14 describe God as a Father? _____

_____

_____

_____

What four dimensions describe God's love for us? _____

_____

_____

_____

What did the Apostle Paul pray we would come to know practically for ourselves? _____

_____

_____

_____

In what ways have you seen Christ's love practically, for yourself?

_____

_____

_____

What does God want us to be filled with? _____

_____

_____

_____

In your own words, describe what this means to you. _____

_____

_____

_____

What has God promised to do if we ask? _____

_____

_____

_____

Do you see it? If you desire to experience more of Christ's love in your life, pray this prayer in Ephesians 3 for yourself and others.

Let's continue in our study.

C. KNOWING GOD THE SON—JESUS CHRIST

1. John 17:3 KJV

And this is life eternal, that they might know thee the only true God, and Jesus Christ, whom thou hast sent.

It's true; isn't it? The deep cry of every person's heart is to know God. Jesus described this as the epitome of eternal life.

In your own words, what does knowing the only true God and Jesus Christ mean to you? _____
_____
_____
_____

Each person has a built-in, spiritual craving to know God—particularly Jesus Christ. We are always searching and spiritually restless until we come into relationship with Jesus. If you are restless and dissatisfied and you just know (or desperately hope) there is more to this Christianity thing than you've experienced, you're on the right trail. You have a good itch. The problem is some people spend years scratching the Jesus-itch with everything but Jesus. I know I did. Everything changes the minute you realize that nothing and no one but Jesus can fully satisfy the itch you feel inside. God designed it that way. Coffee won't do it. Big money won't do it. A million followers on Instagram won't do it (I don't have a million followers, so I am only guessing on this one). Whatever you think will scratch your itch, if it isn't Jesus, it won't. But, when you get to the point where you realize that all you want and have ever wanted was to know Jesus, you have arrived at the beginning of the fulfillment of this verse of Scripture—this *is* eternal life, to know Him!

2. Colossians 2:6-9

As you have therefore received Christ Jesus the Lord, so walk in Him, rooted and built up in Him and established in the faith, as you have been taught, abounding in it with thanksgiving. Beware lest anyone cheat you through philosophy and empty deceit, according to the tradition of men, according to the basic principles of the world, and not according to Christ. For in Him dwells all the fullness of the Godhead bodily.

Jesus was the divine revelation of the Father, Son, and Spirit as He walked upon this earth. The fullness of the Godhead dwells where?

_____

_____

_____

This is where our minds go tilt. It's hard to wrap our heads around the oneness of the Father, Jesus, and the Holy Spirit, while they are still three Persons. Don't drive yourself to drink trying to figure it out. Just enjoy getting to know the Father, getting to know Jesus, and getting to know the Holy Spirit personally.

Now, let's spend the rest of this chapter and most of the book focused on knowing the Holy Spirit better. Who is the Holy Spirit? What is He like? What is His role? How do we get to know Him better?

D. KNOWING GOD THE HOLY SPIRIT

If you could meet and spend one year of quality time with any modern day world changer, whom would you choose? If you could live with the most loving, compassionate, and merciful person in the world, whom would you select? If you could interview one the most powerful people in the world, whom would that be? If you could go on vacation with one of the most talented, humorous and creative people you know, whom would you want to be around? If you could work on a project with one of the wisest or wealthiest people on earth, whom would you choose?

While it would be great to rub shoulders with these types of amazing people, there is actually someone on the earth who is even greater! He is much more loving, influential, powerful, talented, fun, creative, wise, and loaded with riches; and He *wants* to spend time with *you!* More than that, He wants to live in and through you!

The Holy Spirit is that Greater One!

He is the most loving, influential, powerful, talented, creative, fun, wise, and wealthy person on earth—not to mention His many other eternal attributes. Knowing the Holy Spirit is the beginning of a great adventure with God. The Spirit empowered life is the secret for overcoming a predictable, natural, boring, senses-ruled life and for living the dynamic, faith-filled, satisfied, significant and supernatural life. *(Boom!)*

Listen to what Jesus said about knowing the Holy Spirit.

John 16:7, AMPC

However, I am telling you nothing but the truth when I say it is profitable (good, expedient, advantageous) for you that I go away. Because if I do not go away, the Comforter (Counselor, Helper, Advocate, Intercessor, Strengthener, Standby) will not come to you [into close fellowship with you]; but if I go away, I will send Him to you [to be in close fellowship with you].

Jesus said it was profitable, good, expedient, and advantageous for us that He went away to heaven so He could send the Holy Spirit to be in close fellowship with us. I don't know about you, but the idea of walking on earth with Jesus in the flesh sounds pretty good to me. Can you imagine what it would be like to literally see Jesus every day? The disciples had this privilege. They could talk to Him; ask Him questions; eat meals together; see Him teach, preach, heal, and perform miracles for people as they traveled the dusty roads of life and ministry together. What a life!

So, when Jesus said it would be even better when He was not on the earth, they had to be thinking, "Right! You're the only one who can multiply bread and fish, heal the sick, and open blind eyes. You are the only one who can walk on water (well, with the exception of Peter for three seconds), so, how is this going to be better?"

Of course, Jesus was right. He was trying to get them to see that in the same way they related to Him daily, they (and the rest of humanity) would be able to do the very same thing with, by, and through the Holy Spirit. It was definitely going to be profitable, good, expedient, and advantageous for them (and us) when He sent the Holy Spirit because then, it wouldn't be just the twelve who got to spend personal time with the Lord asking questions, eating meals, ministering to people, and traveling through life. This personal relationship with Jesus would be available for everyone through the ages by the power of the Holy Spirit!

And that's not all! The Holy Spirit wouldn't just be with everyone, as Jesus was with the disciples. He would be *in* and *upon* everyone who was born of and filled with the Spirit, something Jesus in the flesh could never do. Jesus could be in one place at one time, and that limited the number of people who could get close to Him. The Holy Spirit could be everywhere at all times, thus opening the door for everyone everywhere to get close to the Lord.

They didn't know it then, but Jesus was telling them that after He left the earth, everyone would have the chance to be born of the Spirit and filled with the Spirit. And that would be a game changer.

Let's look at this good, expedient, and advantageous life with the Holy Spirit.

The Holy Spirit is the third person of the Godhead. He is not a power, vapor, force, or an "it." He is a Spirit. A Holy Spirit. He is a person. He is just as much God as the Father and Jesus. The Holy Spirit wants to empower, commune, guide, and lead us every day of our lives.

When we know Him, it's easy to flow with Him.

Knowing equals flowing! (Another tidbit worth remembering!)

Now, let's pitch a tent and camp out in a few scriptures to get to know our dear intimate friend, the Holy Spirit.

E. 15 THINGS WE SHOULD KNOW ABOUT THE HOLY SPIRIT AND HIS FLOW

1. He Wants An Intimate Friendship with Us.

2 Corinthians 13:14, Message

The amazing grace of the Master, Jesus Christ, the extravagant love of God, the intimate friendship of the Holy Spirit, be with all of you.

What three things does God want us to experience with Him?

_____

_____

Describe what the amazing grace of the Master, Jesus Christ, means to you. _____

_____

_____

_____

Describe what the extravagant love of God means to you. _____

_____

_____

_____

Describe what the intimate friendship with the Holy Spirit means to you. _____

_____

_____

_____

There's something warm and endearing and loving about the *intimate friendship* phrase. One version says, "communion of the Holy Spirit." You get the idea that He wants to be with us, so close to us, that we could be cherished friends of the Holy Spirit. Indeed, we can.

On a small, dog-like scale, this has hit home recently. You'll hear more about our sweet little tea-cup poodle, Jonesie later in the book, but I want to mention her now (since two minutes have passed and I haven't talked about her yet). Here's the thing, Jonesie can't speak a word, and she only weighs two pounds, but she has stolen my and my husband Jeff's hearts. We just like to be with her. And by with, I mean with and or touching. She goes everywhere with us, including to our office every day. She is usually sitting on my lap, my husband's lap, or laying in one of her many plushy beds at our feet. How this happened, I can't even tell you. We were totally not dog people a mere ten months ago! But this little girl came into our lives, and we just like to be with her. We act like total goons when we talk to her (and so do you dear reader, if you are a dog person). "Come here Jonesie baby girl. You little peanut, monkey face. How's my Jonesie? [voice octave going higher] How's my Jonesie? You little snuggle bunny, come sit with me." Then without notice, we will randomly bust into her theme song and sing it straight into her face, "Hey there Jonesie girl . . . Jonesie girl. You're the only dog for me . . ." What kind of weirdos are we? Singing to a dog? We are just smitten, that's all. And guess what? The Holy Spirit is smitten with us. He loves us and feels a whole lot more for us, His intimate and cherished friends, than we feel for Jonesie! I bet He has a theme song for us, which He probably sings over us with joy every day. (Hello, Zephaniah 3:17. All day. Every day. Look it up.)

2. He Leads Us

Romans 8:14

For as many as are led by the Spirit of God, these are sons of God.

As a child of God, what can you expect the Holy Spirit to do for you? _____

_____

_____

_____

In what ways has the Holy Spirit led you recently? _____

_____

_____

_____

Check the areas where He has led you recently, and describe how He led you by His hand:

____ in a relationship _____

____ in an important decision _____

____ in your finances _____

____ in a career decision _____

____ in your health _____

____ in your family _____

____ in your relationship with Him _____

____ in your ministry _____

____ in other _____

For a moment, let's think about being led by the Holy Spirit in terms of ballroom dancing. If you've ever watched professional ballroom dancers doing the waltz or foxtrot, it's easy to see the flow between them. One person leads, and the other person follows and together, they flow beautifully. (And that, my friends, is the basic point of this whole book. The End.)

Years ago, my husband and I took a ballroom dance class for fun. (Think two leggy flamingos trying to not trip over each other.) One of the first things we learned is that it was my job to follow his lead. That took some getting used to because it requires trust (not my strong suit). When I felt off balance or like I was about to stumble, rather than trusting Jeff, I tried to lead the dance. This led to our tangled flamingo legs moving to an offbeat stutter step. How in the world do you follow the leader in dancing when you have no idea where he is going? I seriously wondered. On top of that I was not allowed to look at my feet because I was supposed to be looking regal as I stared over Jeff's right shoulder.

I couldn't figure out how to follow Jeff's lead, which must have been obvious to our instructor as he ordered me, "Follow the hand!" What hand? Gently he explained, "Jeff's job is to lead you with his hand and you are to follow wherever his hand directs you to go." Well, surprise, surprise. When I focused on following Jeff's hand, he led, spun, and moved me around that dance floor like we'd just won *Dancing with the Stars*. (Dancing with the Stars from Mars, in our case!)

I think there are many parallels in flowing with the Holy Spirit. If we focus less on trying to be the leader or on what we need to do, and we focus more on following the leading of His hand, we will find the flow of the Spirit.

3. He Comforts Us and So Much More

John 16:7 AMPC

However, I am telling you nothing but the truth when I say it is profitable (good, expedient, advantageous) for you that I go away. Because if I do not go away, the Comforter (Counselor, Helper, Advocate, Intercessor, Strengthener, Standby) will not come to you [into close fellowship with you]; but if I go away, I will send Him to you [to be in close fellowship with you].

Remember this verse? Once again, let's look at why it was good, expedient, advantageous, and profitable for Jesus to go to heaven and send the Holy Spirit.

The word "comforter" translated is from the Greek word *parakletos*, which literally means "called to one's aid."[2] According to Thayer's Greek Lexicon, one of the meanings of *parakletos* is, "in the widest sense, a helper, succorer, aider, assistant; said of the Holy Spirit destined to take the place of Christ with the apostles (after his ascension to the Father), to lead them to a deeper knowledge of gospel truth . . ."[3]

The classic Amplified Bible brings this out by defining comforter as our counselor, helper, advocate, intercessor, strengthener, and standby.

In your own words, how would you define these words that describe the Holy Spirit and His relationship with you?

Comforter _____

Counselor _____

Helper _____

Advocate _____

Intercessor _____

Strengthener _____

Standby _____

Don't run past this passage. The Holy Spirit will comfort you when no one understands what's breaking your heart. He will counsel you when other counselors have given up. He will help you overcome being socially awkward by showing you how to find a friend and how to be a friend. He will go to bat for you. He will stand in the gap for you. He will strengthen you when you want to quit, and He will be on standby to help you kick into another gear. If you ask the Spirit to help you meditate on each one of these words, I believe He will meet you in a rich and deep way.

According to the last part of this verse, what type of relationship does the Holy Spirit want with us? _____

_____

_____

What does having a close fellowship with the Holy Spirit look like to you? _____

_____

_____

The Holy Spirit is better than having the best 24/7 life coach. He not only coaches, counsels, helps, comforts, and strengthens us in the spectacular, supernatural aspects of our lives. He also helps us in the mundane, like the daily grind at work, finding friends when you move to a new city, loving your mother-in-law who was surely cloned from Cruella De Vil, figuring out what to make from a box of pasta, two eggs, and a can of tuna, raising teenagers who think they're smarter than God, caring for aging parents who still want to drive, bringing sexy back to your marriage, and living a disciplined life of good choices. In other words, this life empowered by the Spirit will benefit everything in your existence (#truthbomb).

Don't get me wrong, the Spirit–empowered life doesn't mean that everything will be a bed of roses. In fact, some seasons will feel like a bed of thorns, downright difficult, troublesome, and full of stress and pressure and persecution. It does mean, however, that there will be a divine flow of the Father's love, Christ's power, and Holy Spirit's help to cause us to triumph over any affliction or difficulty.

4. He Guides Us into All Truth

John 16:8-13 AMPC

And when He comes, He will convict and convince the world and bring demonstration to it about sin and about righteousness (uprightness of heart and right standing with God) and about judgment: About sin, because they do not believe in Me [trust in, rely on, and adhere to Me]; About righteousness (uprightness of heart and right standing with God), because I go to My Father, and you will see Me no longer; About judgment, because the ruler (evil genius, prince) of this world [Satan] is judged and condemned and sentence already is passed upon him. I have still many things to say to you, but you are not able to bear them or to take them upon you or to grasp them now. But when He, the Spirit of Truth (the Truth-giving Spirit) comes, He will guide you into all the Truth (the whole, full Truth). For He will not speak His own message [on His own authority]; but He will tell whatever He hears [from the Father].

What three things does the Holy Spirit do in the hearts of those in the world who do not yet know Jesus? _____

_____

_____

One of the roles of the Holy Spirit is to draw us to Jesus.

Do you remember His work in your own life? Describe it. _____

_____

_____

The Holy Spirit tells, convinces, rebukes, and convicts those who don't yet know the Lord to turn their hearts to Jesus.

In verse 13, what is the Holy Spirit called? _____

_____

_____

What does the Holy Spirit do? _____

_____

_____

How would you describe a guide? _____

_____

_____

In a world where lies, falsehoods, and embellishments abound, why is it comforting to know the Holy Spirit will always lead you to the truth—the whole, full truth? _____

_____

_____

I don't know about you, but I have to put on my big girl pants to hear the truth. I want the truth and nothing but the truth, until I get the truth. Then I want a lollipop and my pacifier. The truth definitely sets us free, but first it ticks us off (as someone on Pinterest once said).

5. He Reveals Things to Us

John 16:13-15 AMPC

He will announce *and* declare to you the things that are to come [that will happen in the future]. He will honor *and* glorify Me, because He will take of (receive, draw upon) what is Mine and will reveal (declare, disclose, transmit) it to you. Everything that the Father has is Mine. That is what I meant when I said that He [the Spirit] will take the things that are Mine and will reveal (declare, disclose, transmit) it to you.

What will the Holy Spirit announce and declare to us? _____

_____

_____

When it comes to your life and future, what can you expect the Holy Spirit to do for you? _____

_____

_____

Describe a time when He showed you things to come: _____

_____

_____

It's a great blessing to know the Holy Spirit reveals and shows us things to come. He will always give you a heads up when you need to have a revelation about present concerns and future things. You may not know every detail about things to come, but you will have a sense or an awareness of future things. For example, if they are going to be downsizing at your place of employment, there is a very good chance the Holy Spirit will give you an advance notification that something is up so you can pray or prepare.

Or let's say one of your kids who you think is basically perfect has actually (unbeknownst to you) begun to hang out with the wrong crowd and one day the Holy Spirit prompts you to check the little darling's backpack where you find some incriminating contraband. (Insert sound of pressure cooker releasing steam.) You calmly and in a Christ-like way ring your dear child's neck, take the car keys, the cell phone, and ground your angel for the next 12 years in an effort to head off this short-lived rebellious streak. (Hypothetically speaking, of course!)

Who does the Holy Spirit always honor and glorify? _____

_____

_____

Remember, the Holy Spirit always glorifies Jesus. Jesus is at the center of everything the Holy Spirit does.

The Holy Spirit is a revealer. He uncovers things that we need to see or know.

Have you experienced this in your life? Describe it. _____

_____

_____

_____

What else will the Holy Spirit reveal to us? _____

_____

_____

_____

Can you see the Godhead—Father, Jesus, and Holy Spirit—all mentioned in this passage? _____

_____

_____

According to this passage, what does the Father do? _____

_____

_____

_____

What does Jesus do? _____

_____

_____

What does the Spirit do for us? _____

_____

_____

How does the flow of communication work from heaven to us?

_____

_____

How would you define these words that describe the way the Holy Spirit communicates to us:

Tell _____   Give _____

Announce _____   Declare _____

Reveal _____   Declare _____

Disclose _____   Transmit _____

What do you need the Holy Spirit to reveal to you in this season of your life? _____

_____

_____

The Holy Spirit always reveals things to us that are in line with His Word, His character, His love and His grace. He would never reveal things to hurt us, scare us, gossip about us, or mislead us.

6. He Is Not Only with Us, He Is In Us

John 14:16-17, AMPC

I will ask the Father, and He will give you another Comforter (Counselor, Helper, Intercessor, Advocate, Strengthener, and Standby), that He may remain with you forever—The Spirit of Truth, Whom the world cannot receive (welcome, take to its heart), because it does not see Him or know and recognize Him. But you know *and* recognize Him, for He lives with you [constantly] and will be in you. I will not leave you as orphans [comfortless, desolate, bereaved, forlorn, helpless]; I will come [back] to you.

The Holy Spirit isn't just with us, He is _____ us.

The Holy Spirit is described in many ways. List all the ways He is described in this passage. _____

_____

_____

Concerning our relationship with the Holy Spirit, we are to _____ and _____ Him, for he lives with us!

In what condition did Jesus say He would not leave us? _____

_____

_____

Notice, Jesus told His disciples (and us) that after He died on the cross and rose from the dead, He would not leave them as orphans, but He would send One just like Him to be *with* them and *in* them. And, when He sent this One, it would be better for them (and us) than if He had stayed. So, He did just that, He sent the Holy Spirit.

How was it better? In multiplied, multi-generational ways! In whatever ways the disciples interacted with Jesus during His three years of ministry on earth—walking, talking, sitting, eating, praying, preaching, teaching, healing, explaining, partnering, and doing life—the Holy Spirit would now take the baton and do the exact same thing *for* them and us, not for three years but for thousands of years! Whatever they saw Jesus do, say, pray, heal, multiply, rebuke, ask, answer, comfort, forgive, hold, defend, or love during those three years, the Holy Spirit would now take that baton and do the very same thing *to* and *through* them and us for the next thousands of years! This is the real time, present-tense ministry of the Holy Spirit. Jesus was right; this is better!

Seriously, reread that last paragraph, it's loaded! (Another #truthbomb!)

7. Our Bodies Are His Temple

1 Corinthians 6:19

Or do you not know that your body is the temple of the Holy Spirit *who* is in you, whom you have from God, and you are not your own?

What is our body? _____
_____
_____

Where does the Holy Spirit reside? _____
_____
_____

When we receive Jesus as our Lord, the Holy Spirit comes to dwell in our spirit, which is in our body. He takes up residence in us!

8. He Is Greater than Anyone

1 John 4:2-4

By this you know the Spirit of God: Every spirit that confesses that Jesus Christ has come in the flesh is of God, and every spirit that does not confess that Jesus Christ has come in the flesh is not of God. And this is the spirit of the Antichrist, which you have heard was coming, and is now already in the world. You are of God, little children, and have overcome them, because He who is in you is greater than he who is in the world.

How can we recognize the Spirit of God? _____
_____
_____

According to verse 4, Who lives in you? _____

_____

_____

Is anyone or anything greater than the Spirit who lives in you? __

_____

_____

The greatest One of all lives in you, and He wants to have an intimate friendship with you!

You + the Holy Spirit = Overcomer Extraordinaire

9. He Produces Good Fruit in Our Lives

Galatians 5:22-23 NLT

But the Holy Spirit produces this kind of fruit in our lives: love, joy, peace, patience, kindness, goodness, faithfulness, gentleness, and self-control.

Being born of and filled with the Spirit will not only give you the power you need to live as a witness for Christ, it will also produce good fruit in your life.

As we get to know the Holy Spirit, what type of fruit should become evident in our lives? _____

_____

_____

In your own words, what does this fruit look like?

Love _____

Joy _____

Peace _____

Patience _____

Kindness _____

Goodness _____

Faithfulness _____

Gentleness _____

Self-Control _____

Can you see it, friend?

10. He Teaches Us

John 14:26

But the Helper, the Holy Spirit, whom the Father will send in My name, He will teach you all things, and bring to your remembrance all things that I said to you.

In what ways does the Holy Spirit help us? _____

_____

_____

How would you describe His role as a helper? _____

_____

_____

What does the Holy Spirit teach us? _____

_____

_____

What does the Holy Spirit remind us of? _____

_____

_____

11. He Anoints Us

1 John 2:20

But you have an anointing from the Holy One, and you know all things.

What does the Holy Spirit give us? _____

_____

_____

What does the anointing help us to do? _____

_____

_____

The Holy Spirit helps us to know all things! That doesn't mean we become all-knowing geniuses, but it does mean that we can count on Him to anoint us to know the truth about everything we need to know, when we need to know it.

What is an *anointing*? When something was anointed in the Old Testament, grease or oil was smeared on it to bring life, refreshment, soothing and healing, or to set it apart for God's purposes. What does that mean for us?

When the Holy Spirit anoints a person, an idea, a message, a song, or anything else, there will be life in it! It will bring warmth, a refreshing and soothing or comfortable knowing to our spirit. It's easy to say "amen" to things that are anointed.

During our Michigan winters, I anoint my face almost every night with coconut oil, and it brings an instant sense of soothing and refreshment. We have received an anointing from the Holy Spirit so that when we need to know things, there will be a soothing and refreshing sense within our spirit as we discern His direction.

Have you ever tried to move forward with someone or something but there was no life in it? It just felt dead, like you were forcing it. Did you feel as cold as ice about it? Or as one of our mentors would say, "Did it feel like you were sledding down a dirt hill?" The lack of anointing is often indicative that the Holy Spirit is not in it.

For example, a few years ago I had a desire to get a puppy. (Yes, it's another Jonesie story!) I should tell you, I'd had this desire about once a year. Over the years when our kids were little, we had tried to have dogs, but the timing was never quite right. We'd had three dogs for a few months each, but we ended up giving Sparky, Grace, and Faith to other families who were anointed to have them.

As we approached an empty nest, I found this new desire for a puppy growing stronger within me. Naturally, I didn't think there was any way we could get a puppy. We were just too busy. We traveled too much. It wouldn't be fair to the puppy. However, every time I thought about getting a dog, I felt this warmth inside. I felt a soothing love in my heart for this puppy that we did not have and did not plan on getting!

Eventually, I realized that the Holy Spirit was anointing me to get a puppy. (It might sound crazy, but I needed to be anointed to get a puppy if it was ever going to happen!) So we found our little baby girl, Jonesie, a teacup poodle about the size of a squirrel. My husband and I fell in love with her instantly—a true sign of the anointing since my husband wanted to get a pit bull. But now, I am not sure who loves Jonesie more—me or my husband and his 6'6" self. She is the absolute sweetest dog ever, and I had no idea I could love a dog so much. The anointing makes you do things you never thought you could do (like buying a dog stroller at a thrift store and proudly using it in public). Don't judge. Can I get witness from my anointed dog-loving friends?

12. He Gives Life to Our Bodies

Romans 8:11

But if the Spirit of Him who raised Jesus from the dead dwells in you, He who raised Christ from the dead will also give life to your mortal bodies through His Spirit who dwells in you.

What does the Spirit do to help our mortal bodies in this life and in the resurrection? _____
_____
_____

If you are not feeling well physically, what could you expect the Holy Spirit to do for you? _____
_____
_____

13. He Speaks to Our Spirit

Romans 8:16, ERV

And the Spirit himself speaks to our spirits and makes us sure that we are God's children.

What part of us does the Spirit speak to? _____
_____
_____

What does He reassure us of? _____
_____
_____

According to 1 Thessalonians 5:23, we are a three-part person: "I pray God your whole spirit and soul and body be preserved blameless unto the coming of our Lord Jesus Christ." That is, we *are* a spirit, we *have* a soul, and we *live* in a body. It's always good to listen on the inside, in your spirit (also known as the inner man or the hidden man of the heart) to hear what the Spirit is saying to us.

14. He Prays with Us

Romans 8:26-28

Likewise the Spirit also helps in our weaknesses. For we do not know what we should pray for as we ought, but the Spirit Himself makes intercession for us with groanings which cannot be uttered. Now He who searches the hearts knows what the mind of the Spirit *is*, because He makes intercession for the saints according to *the will of* God. And we know that all things work together for good to those who love God, to those who are the called according to *His* purpose.

What does the Holy Spirit promise to help us with? _____

_____

_____

When we don't know how to pray, what does the Holy Spirit help us do? _____

_____

_____

How does He help us pray and make intercession? _____

_____

_____

What does the Holy Spirit know? _____
_____
_____

What are we promised if we allow the Holy Spirit to work together with us in prayer? _____
_____
_____

We'll talk more about this in our next chapter.

15. He Strengthens Us

Ephesians 3:14-16 AMPC

For this reason [seeing the greatness of this plan by which you are built together in Christ], I bow my knees before the Father of *our Lord Jesus Christ*, for Whom every family in heaven and on earth is named [that Father from Whom all fatherhood takes its title and derives its name]. May He grant you out of the rich treasury of His glory to be strengthened *and* reinforced with mighty power in the inner man by the [Holy] Spirit [Himself indwelling your innermost being and personality].

What does the Holy Spirit do for us? _____
_____
_____

Describe how and where He strengthens us? _____
_____
_____

This is a great prayer to pray for yourself when you need the Lord's inner strengthening.

When we learn how to flow with the Holy Spirit, He strengthens us to walk *through* the valley of the shadow of death, to get the victory *over* challenges we face, and to become more and more transformed in how we think and act to reflect our true identities as His representatives to the world. He enlarges our world and reinforces us with His power to share our faith in genuine ways—caring enough to pray for others, being compassionate enough to reach out to those in need, generous enough to give to those less fortunate, and empowered enough to do something about something!

Dear friends, can you see why I wanted to shout "Surprise" at the beginning of this book? Isn't He wonderful? I hope you are already experiencing more of His indwelling presence as you go through this study. Let's venture on and look at what it means to be filled with the Spirit?

NOTES

[1] "Genesis chapter 1 (KJV)," *Blue Letter Bible*, accessed Nov 12, 2015 https://www.blueletterbible.org/lang/lexicon/lexicon.cfm?Strongs=H259&t=KJV

[2] *Thayer's Greek Lexicon*, S.V. "Paraklétos," accessed Nov 12, 2015. http://biblehub.com/greek/3875.htm

[3] Ibid.

JOURNAL ENTRY

To get the most out of this chapter, take a few moments to journal your thoughts and/or prayers.

_____

_____

SESSION 2:
BEING FILLED WITH
THE HOLY SPIRIT

———— ◆◈◆ ————

We all know the dread of a mobile phone whose battery is on the verge of dying, right? We do whatever we can to preserve the smallest flow of power in our mobile devices, don't we? Have you searched for an outlet in a coffee shop or airport terminal like a ninja? Do you wake up in the middle of the night like it's your job, just to plug in your phone?

What if we approached being full of the Spirit with the same desire and tenacity we have for keeping our mobile devices charged?

Thousands of years ago, the prophet Zechariah described God's program to empower His people: "'Not by might nor by power, but by My Spirit,' says the LORD of hosts" (Zechariah 4:6).

Two thousand years ago, Jesus confirmed God's plan to empower His people: "But you shall receive power when the Holy Spirit has come upon you; and you shall be witnesses to Me in Jerusalem, and in all Judea and Samaria, and to the end of the earth" (Acts 1:8).

So, how does this actually work? How do we cooperate with the Holy Spirit to keep our spiritual batteries fully charged? Let's look at two of the most important experiences available for every believer:

1) The initial experience of being born of the Spirit

2) The subsequent experience of being filled with the Spirit.

A. WHAT DOES IT MEAN TO BE BORN OF AND FILLED WITH THE HOLY SPIRIT?

The Bible describes two very important facets of being empowered by the Holy Spirit—being born of and filled with the Spirit. It's important to understand the Biblical difference between these two significant experiences.

When we believe and receive Jesus as our Lord, we are born of the Spirit. We become born again believers, and the Spirit comes to live *within* our spirit.

When we thirst for more of God and receive the infilling or baptism of the Spirit, we are filled with the Spirit. The Holy Spirit comes *upon* our spirit, and we are empowered for service.

Every believer is entitled to these two experiences with the Holy Spirit.

1. Born of the Spirit—The Spirit Within

First and foremost is the experience of being born of the Spirit. This is known as being born-again, being saved, receiving the new birth or second birth, being made a new creation in Christ, and/or becoming a Christian or a fully devoted follower of Jesus Christ. When we receive Jesus by believing in our heart and confessing with our mouth that Jesus is Lord and that God raised Him from the dead, we receive the gift of salvation or eternal life. At that moment, we are *born of* the Spirit.

In basic terms, what happens is a supernatural rebirth of our spiritually dead human spirit. The Holy Spirit recreates our human spirit, then He dwells *within* our now recreated, regenerated, born-again spirit. In this process, He completely removes our old fallen nature and replaces it with a new nature that is righteous in His sight (2 Corinthians 5:17). We literally become "new creatures in Christ."

Let's look at two other scriptures that describe being born of the Spirit. Make note of and/or circle these important phrases "born of the Spirit" and "the Spirit within."

John 3:5

Jesus answered, "Most assuredly, I say to you, unless one is born of water and the Spirit, he cannot enter the kingdom of God."

Jesus said that unless a person is born of water and ____ he cannot enter the kingdom of God.

John 14:17

The Spirit of truth, whom the world cannot receive, because it neither sees Him nor knows Him; but you know Him, for He dwells with you and will be in you.

Jesus said the Holy Spirit would dwell ____ us and shall be ____ us.

2. Filled with the Spirit—The Spirit Upon

Second, and very important, is the experience subsequent to salvation known in the Scriptures as being filled with the Holy Spirit, receiving the Holy Spirit, being baptized with the Spirit, or the Spirit coming upon our spirit. All of these terms refer to the same experience. When this happens, the Holy Spirit who lives within our spirit now comes upon our spirit and endues us with power for living the Christian life, for being a witness for Christ and for serving the Lord. Let's look at several examples of this in the Word. Make note of these phrases "filled with the Spirit" and "the Spirit upon," which describe the same thing.

Acts 1:8

But you shall receive power when the Holy Spirit has come upon you; and you shall be witnesses to Me in Jerusalem, and in all Judea and Samaria, and to the end of the earth.

Jesus said that the Holy Spirit would come ____ us. (This is different than the Holy Spirit within us.)

Acts 2:4

And they were all filled with the Holy Spirit and began to speak with other tongues, as the Spirit gave them utterance.

After the believers were____ with the Spirit, they began to speak in tongues as the Spirit gave them utterance.

Can you see the various words and phrases being used for the two experiences of being born of the Spirit and filled with the Spirit?

Born of the Spirit = the Spirit within our spirit

Filled with the Spirit = the Spirit upon our spirit

B. WHAT'S THE DIFFERENCE BETWEEN BEING BORN OF AND FILLED WITH THE HOLY SPIRIT?

The difference between being born of the Spirit (the experience of salvation where the Spirit comes to live within a believer) and being filled with the Spirit (the experience of being baptized with the Spirit where the Spirit comes upon a believer) is examined in the following scriptures.

1. Born of the Spirit

1 Corinthians 12:13

For by one Spirit we were all baptized into one body—whether Jews or Greeks, whether slaves or free—and have all been made to drink into one Spirit.

When we are born of the Spirit, it's He, the Holy Spirit, Who baptizes or places us into the Body of Christ.

Who is the baptizer in this verse? _____

Who does the Holy Spirit baptize? _____

What does the Holy Spirit baptize us into? _____

Baptized: It means "to dip into" or "to immerse."[1]

We can see from these scriptures that when we are born of Him, the Holy Spirit baptizes us and places us into the Body of Christ immediately. The Holy Spirit transfers us from the kingdom of darkness into the kingdom of God's dear Son (Colossians 1:13). This is something that happens automatically to every believer of Jesus Christ when they are born again.

2. Filled with the Spirit

Luke 3:16

John answered, saying to all, "I indeed baptize you with water; but One mightier than I is coming, whose sandal strap I am not worthy to loose. He will baptize you with the Holy Spirit and fire."

When we are filled with the Spirit, it's Jesus who baptizes or immerses us in the Holy Spirit.

Who was John speaking about as the baptizer in the last part of the verse? _____

Who would Jesus baptize? _____

What does Jesus baptized us in or with? _____

When we are filled with the Spirit, the Lord Jesus then baptizes us with the Holy Spirit. This happens subsequent to our being born again. This baptism of the Spirit is available to every believer who desires more of God. In fact, Jesus, in Acts 1:4-5, commands all believers to be baptized in the Holy Spirit.

C. COMPARING THE TWO EXPERIENCES

Let's look at numerous passages of Scripture about the life of Jesus and other believers to compare the experience of being born of the Spirit and filled with the Spirit. First, we are born of the Spirit when we receive Jesus as Lord and the Holy Spirit comes to live *within* us. Then, we are to be filled with the Spirit after we receive salvation and the Holy Spirit comes *upon* our spirit.

Place the words "born of the Spirit" or "filled with the Spirit" in the blank space after the scriptures to indicate which experience is depicted in the verse. You may notice a pattern.

1. Jesus

Matthew 1:18-20

Now the birth of Jesus Christ was as follows: After His mother Mary was betrothed to Joseph, before they came together, she was found with child of the Holy Spirit. Then Joseph her husband, being a just *man*, and not wanting to make her a public example, was minded to put her away secretly. But while he thought about these things, behold, an angel of the Lord appeared to him in a dream, saying, "Joseph, son of David, do not be afraid to take to you Mary your wife, for that which is conceived in her is of the Holy Spirit."

Matthew 3:16

When He had been baptized, Jesus came up immediately from the water; and behold, the heavens were opened to Him, and He saw the Spirit of God descending like a dove and alighting upon Him.

---

2. The Disciples

John 20:21-22

So Jesus said to them again, "Peace to you! As the Father has sent Me, I also send you." And when He had said this,

He breathed on *them*, and said to them, "Receive the Holy Spirit."

Acts 1:2-5

until the day in which He was taken up, after He through the Holy Spirit had given commandments to the apostles whom He had chosen, to whom He also presented Himself alive after His suffering by many infallible proofs, being seen by them during forty days and speaking of the things pertaining to the kingdom of God. And being assembled together with *them*, He commanded them not to depart from Jerusalem, but to wait for the Promise of the Father, "which," *He said*, "you have heard from Me; for John truly baptized with water, but you shall be baptized with the Holy Spirit not many days from now."

3. The Samaritans

Acts 8:5, 12

Then Philip went down to the city of Samaria and preached Christ to them. But when they believed Philip as he preached the things concerning the kingdom of God and the name of Jesus Christ, both men and women were baptized.

Acts 8:14-17

Now when the apostles who were at Jerusalem heard that Samaria had received the word of God, they sent Peter and John to them, who, when they had come down, prayed for them that they might receive the Holy Spirit. For as yet He had fallen upon none of them. They had only been baptized in the name of the Lord Jesus. Then they laid hands on them, and they received the Holy Spirit.

4. The Gentiles

Acts 11:1, 17

Now the apostles and brethren who were in Judea heard that the Gentiles had also received the word of God. If therefore God gave them the same gift as *He gave* us when we believed on the Lord Jesus Christ, who was I that I could withstand God?

(In Acts 11, Peter describes what happened to Cornelius and the Gentile believers in Acts 10.)

Acts 10:44-46

While Peter was still speaking these words, the Holy Spirit fell upon all those who heard the word. And those of the circumcision who believed were astonished, as many as came with Peter, because the gift of the Holy Spirit had been poured out on the Gentiles also. For they heard them speak with tongues and magnify God.

5. The Ephesians

Acts 19:1-5

And it happened, while Apollos was at Corinth, that Paul, having passed through the upper regions, came to Ephesus. And finding some disciples he said to them, "Did you receive the Holy Spirit when you believed?" So they said to him, "We have not so much as heard whether there is a Holy Spirit." And he said to them, "Into what then were you baptized?" So they said, "Into John's baptism." Then Paul said, "John indeed baptized with a baptism of repentance, saying to the people that they should believe on Him who would come after him, that is, on Christ Jesus." When they heard this, they were baptized in the name of the Lord Jesus.

Acts 19:6

And when Paul had laid hands on them, the Holy Spirit came upon them, and they spoke with tongues and prophesied.

From these passages, can you see the two experiences for every believer? First, believers are born of the Spirit then subsequently filled with the Spirit and empowered for serving the Lord.

One simple illustration I've heard to describe the difference between these two experiences is this. Imagine a glass of water that is full and overflowing. Let's say that glass is a Christian. Having all that water *within* the glass means the glass has been born of the Spirit and the Spirit is flowing within and even overflowing from it. As wonderful as that is, this glass is not yet baptized or filled with the Spirit! However, if we submerge that full cup into an ocean of water, that glass would be both born of and filled with the Spirit. It would have the water *within* and *upon* it, splashing all over the place!

6. The Woman at the Well and the People at the Feast

John 4:7-15 KJV

There cometh a woman of Samaria to draw water: Jesus saith unto her, Give me to drink. (For his disciples were gone away unto the city to buy meat.) Then saith the woman of Samaria unto him, How is it that thou, being a Jew, askest drink of me, which am a woman of Samaria? for the Jews have no dealings with the Samaritans. Jesus answered and said unto her, If thou knewest the gift of God, and who it is that saith to thee, Give me to drink; thou wouldest have asked of him, and he would have given thee living water. The woman saith unto him, Sir, thou hast nothing to draw with, and the well is deep: from whence then hast thou that living water? Art thou greater than our father Jacob, which gave us the well, and drank thereof himself, and his children, and his cattle? Jesus answered and said unto her, Whosoever drinketh of this water shall thirst again: But whosoever drinketh of the water that I shall give him shall never thirst; but the water that I shall give him shall be in him a well of water springing up into everlasting life. The woman saith unto him, Sir, give me this water, that I thirst not, neither come hither to draw.

Jesus described being born of the Spirit. What metaphor did He use? _____

_____

How did Jesus describe this supernatural well? _____

_____

_____

John 7:37-39

On the last day, that great *day* of the feast, Jesus stood and cried out, saying, "If anyone thirsts, let him come to Me and drink. He who believes in Me, as the Scripture has said, out of his heart will flow rivers of living water." But this He spoke concerning the Spirit, whom those believing in Him would receive; for the Holy Spirit was not yet *given*, because Jesus was not yet glorified.

Jesus described being filled with the Spirit. What metaphor did He use? _____

How did Jesus describe this supernatural river? _____

Now, let me check in with you, faithful reader. Is this making sense to you?

Perhaps you've been born of the Spirit for some time, but you are not certain that you've been filled with the Spirit. Maybe you've been a Christian for years and you love the Lord with your whole heart, yet you are still thirsty! Perhaps you find yourself feeling bottled up at times and unable to fully express your heart to God in worship or prayer or in being a witness for Christ? Is there a part of you that longs for freedom to sing? Pray? Worship? Tell others about Jesus? You can tap into a fresh flow of God's Spirit.

If you want rivers of living water to flow from your heart, Jesus has made this available to every believer who is thirsty. Thirst is the only requirement for being filled with the Spirit.

What did Jesus tell those who are thirsty?_____

What did He say would result? _____

Are you thirsty for more of God? _____

It's interesting to note that Jesus gave us two illustrations regarding being born of and filled with the Spirit when He talked about wells to the woman at the well and rivers to the people at the feast. Can you see the benefit of both wells and rivers? When we are born of the Spirit, God puts a well inside of us—a well of living water; a well of salvation. We can draw living water from that well at any time to find refreshment in Christ! When we are filled with the Spirit, God puts rivers inside of us—rivers of living water that flow out from us. We can yield to the Spirit and those rivers will provide a perpetual source of power that refreshes us and enables us to minister to others.

D. HOW CAN I BE FILLED WITH THE HOLY SPIRIT?

God wants every believer to have *both* experiences of being born of the Spirit and being filled with the Spirit.

Of course, if you had to pick between being born of the Spirit and filled with the Spirit, you should pick being born of the Spirit because without being born of the Spirit, you cannot ever see the kingdom of God! But, here's the good news. You don't have to pick one or the other. God wants you to experience both! Assuming you are already born of the Spirit, let's talk about how you can be filled with the Spirit.

1. Ephesians 5:18

And do not be drunk with wine, in which is dissipation; but be filled with the Spirit.

What are God's two words concerning the Holy Spirit? _____

_____

_____

First, let's address one reason why you would want to be filled with the Spirit. You would want to be filled simply because God commands it. He wants us to be filled with the Spirit continually! This scripture literally denotes the idea of continually being filled with the Spirit, to "be filled." To stay full of the Spirit, one would have to receive an initial infilling. Thereafter, we are commanded to continue to be full of the Spirit.

Did you notice the comparison and contrast between being drunk with wine and being filled with the Spirit? It's an interesting metaphor; we'll look at it in our next chapter.

2. Acts 1:8

But you shall receive power when the Holy Spirit has come upon you; and you shall be witnesses to Me in Jerusalem, and in all Judea and Samaria, and to the end of the earth.

What is the purpose for being filled with the Spirit? _____

_____

Want another huge reason to be filled with the Spirit? He is *Thee* power source for a joy-filled, effective, and fruitful Christian life (King James emphasis intended). No joke.

Girls, ever tried using a flat iron on your hair without plugging it in? You could go through all the motions and not one strand of hair will be straightened. Why? Because, there's no power!

Guys, ever tried to scrape—oh, I don't know—about 32 layers of paint off an old windowsill with a handheld steel paint scraper? How about twelve double hung windows? Let's add in the smell of a few gallons of liquid paint remover and your pregnant wife of eight months who is just about to go postal on you. Not a good recipe. (Not that we have experienced this exact thing.) But, plug in the electric power paint stripper, put your wife in a Lazy Boy with a chocolate malt and a pickle and that paint will practically hop off those windows all by itself! What's the difference? Power! (And a happy pregnant wife.)

Power is what the Spirit gives to us. When the Holy Spirit comes upon us, He gives us supernatural power to live for Jesus and to represent the Lord in these three ways . . .

> **First,** The Holy Spirit simply helps us to *not* think of ourselves. He helps us *think about the Lord* and He helps us *focus on others.* (Seems obvious, but, not a default mode for most of us.)
>
> **Second,** He gives us the power, the urge and unction—indeed the exciting anticipation—to share Jesus through our words, our lifestyle, our behavior—and in all that we are.
>
> **Third,** He helps us not be weird. (Which is very subjective, I know.) Rather, He empowers us in our everyday, normal lives, so that we reflect and "preach" Jesus in all that we do. "Witnessing" for Jesus is what we do through our conversations and interactions everyday—and, we need the Holy Spirit's power to do it. Being a witness for Jesus doesn't necessarily mean we need to stand on a street corner wearing a sandwich board with "The End is Near" written all over—although, if I were you, I wouldn't rule it out. (Because as soon as you rule something out, God rules it in. As soon as you tell the Lord what you won't be doing—guess what He'll ask you to do?)

Bottom line? When the Holy Spirit comes upon us, He gives us power to be less self-absorbed and more absorbed with Jesus and others.

He gives us the power and ability to share our faith with those in our sphere of influence and He helps us to not be weird.

3. Luke 11:9-13

So I say to you, ask, and it will be given to you; seek, and you will find; knock, and it will be opened to you. For everyone who asks receives, and he who seeks finds, and to him who knocks it will be opened. If a son asks for bread from any father among you, will he give him a stone? Or if *he asks* for a fish, will he give him a serpent instead of a fish? Or if he asks for an egg, will he offer him a scorpion? *your* heavenly Father give the Holy Spirit to those who ask Him!

What does verse 13 say we can ask the Father for? _____
_____

What do verses 9 and 10 say will happen if you ask? _____
_____

According to verses 11 and 12, if we ask the Father for one thing, will He give us something different? _____
_____

If we ask for the Holy Spirit, what will we receive? _____
_____

As for how to be filled with the Spirit, it's simple. Just ask! When you ask the Father to fill you with the Spirit, the Holy Spirit will come upon your spirit and you will be empowered with Him! God gave the Holy Spirit to all of mankind on the Day of Pentecost, so when you ask the Father to fill you with the Holy Spirit, you are simply saying you want to receive what He has already given to mankind nearly 2,000 years ago.

If you are thirsty and ready to be filled with the Spirit, simply ask, believe, and receive by praying a prayer like this:

Dear Father God, I ask You in Jesus' Name to fill me with the Holy Spirit so that I may receive the fullness of Your Spirit. Lord, I want to have power to be a witness for You. I want to be able to praise You from my innermost being, and I want to speak Your Word boldly. Jesus, I believe You are the baptizer, so I ask You to baptize me in the Spirit. I believe I receive the Holy Spirit coming upon me now. In Jesus' Name. Amen.

Congratulations! Being filled with the Spirit is a marked time in your Christian life. I encourage you to make a record of the date and time. You will appreciate having this documented in the days and years to come!

_____

_____

_____

E. NOW WHAT?

What should you expect once you have been filled with the Spirit? Believe that He has done it, just as He promised.

You receive the infilling of the Holy Spirit by faith (whether you feel a goose bump or not), then you simply yield to Him. You begin to flow with Him. One of the best ways to do that is through praise and prayer and that, my friends, is exactly what we are going to talk about in our next chapter.

But before we move on, you might be one of those people who are already primed and ready to yield to Him now! If you just prayed and received the Holy Spirit and you sense that river bubbling up inside of you, there's no need to delay, go ahead and yield to Him in prayer now.

If you have an urge to thank, praise, and magnify the Lord from your heart in your everyday language *and* in a spiritual language you don't know, this is a manifestation of the Holy Spirit and is the evidence of the Spirit coming upon you. Don't quench this supernatural experience, but rather, yield to the Holy Spirit and let the words He gives you flow from your mouth. You will be praying and/or speaking praises to God in your own language and then in what the Bible calls "other tongues."

Others of you may be thinking, "Whoa! This is all new to me. I want to learn more about being filled with the Spirit and praying in the Spirit in this thing known as tongues." I completely understand. (Refer to "My Story" prior to "Session 1.") Let's continue to study the Word!

Note: Speaking in tongues isn't the only thing that happens when we are filled with the Spirit. There are many benefits to being filled with the Spirit including a new boldness and power in witnessing, receiving more revelation as you study God's Word, and sensing freedom and liberty to praise and worship the Lord. But, because speaking in tongues is often the initial manifestation of being filled with the Spirit, this is where people seem to have the most questions; so let's continue our study in the Word to see what the Bible says about praying in the Holy Spirit—in tongues—in our next chapter.

NOTE

[1]*Blue Letter Bible.* S.V. "Greek Lexicon :: G907 (KJV)," accessed Nov 25, 2015. http://www.blueletterbible.orghttps://www.blueletterbible.org/lang/lexicon/lexicon.cfm

JOURNAL ENTRY:

To get the most out of this chapter, take a few moments to journal your thoughts and/or prayers.

_____

_____

_____

_____

_____

_____

_____

_____

_____

_____

_____

_____

_____

_____

_____

_____

_____

_____

_____

_____

_____

_____

_____

_____

_____

_____

SESSION 3:
PRAYING IN THE HOLY SPIRIT

———◈———

Communication is the oxygen of relationships.

When a bride and groom say "I do" during their wedding vows, it's not the end of their relationship. It's the beginning! After the "I do," they get to enjoy a God-blessed honeymoon, and they spend the rest of their lives getting to know one another and deepening their relationship.

The same is true in our relationship with the Lord. When we say, "I do" to Jesus, it's the beginning of an eternal relationship! To experience a dynamic two-way relationship with the Lord, we must engage in heartfelt communication, prayer, with Him on a regular basis.

As believers, not only does God give us the ability to communicate and pray to Him in our everyday language, but when we are filled with the Spirit, one of the first benefits we receive is the ability to pray in tongues. This is sometimes called praying in the Spirit, a heavenly language, a spiritual language or a prayer language.

So, let's talk about this heavenly prayer language—this speaking in tongues. Unfortunately, tongues often gets a bad rap and becomes the elephant in the room because there is either a lack of knowledge on this topic or because there is confusion and misinformation circulating among Christians. You can put your mind and heart at ease. Speaking in tongues is a good gift from our good God! Speaking and praying in tongues won't put you in a trance, grow hair on your chest, make you cluck like a duck or turn you into a snake charmer. God will never force it upon you, but if you are thirsty and desire to enhance and deepen your relationship and communication with the Lord, open up your heart and let's take a thorough look at God's Word to learn more about this heavenly language of tongues.

A. COMMUNICATING WITH GOD

The Bible describes praying two ways—with our mind and understanding in our everyday language and with our spirit in tongues. Let's look at it.

1. 1 Corinthians 14:15 AMPC

Then what am I to do? I will pray with my spirit [by the Holy Spirit that is within me], but I will also pray [intelligently] with my mind and understanding; I will sing with my spirit [by the Holy Spirit that is within me], but I will sing [intelligently] with my mind and understanding also.

What two ways of prayer does this verse describe? "I will pray with _____, and I will also pray with _____."

So, our mind and understanding have the ability to do what? ____

_____

_____

Our spirit (also known as our heart, inner man, hidden man of the heart, inward man) has the ability to do what? _____

Let's look a little deeper at these two types of prayer.

When we pray with our mind or understanding, we pray in our everyday language. For example, if English is your primary language, that is the language you understand and use when praying with your mind and understanding. When we pray with our mind and understanding, we can pray about many things using the knowledge we have and by asking God for things according to His Word.

Most people pray with their mind and understanding and it's wonderful, but there are limitations to praying with our understanding because we don't have the full knowledge or understanding on many things that need prayer. We also need to pray with our spirit in tongues.

I spent the first three years of my Christian life praying from my heart with my mind and understanding. All of my praying was done in English, since that's the only language I knew. I looked up scriptures and prayed according to what God has promised in His Word. I saw marvelous answers to prayer. God is faithful to His Word. I have journals full of prayers I have written down and answers He has performed. I still enjoy praying with my mind and understanding according to God's Word as He lays things on my heart. While this form of prayer is very fruitful, once I began to pray in the Spirit in tongues, I felt my prayer life had been turbo charged and I was able to pray about things I had no natural understanding on with great precision and according to God's perfect will. Praying in tongues deepened and broadened my prayer life. When we pray with or from our spirit in the heavenly language of tongues, we can pray about things that our mind doesn't know how to pray about.

Being able to pray both with our mind and understanding and with the spirit is the best of both worlds!

(Note: To "pray with the spirit" is a reference to praying in tongues, as you can see from the context of 1 Corinthians 14:14, below.)

2. 1 Corinthians 14:14

For if I pray in a tongue, my spirit prays, but my understanding is unfruitful.

When we pray with our spirit, what language do we speak? _____

_____

What happens to our understanding when we pray in tongues? ___

_____

Our mind doesn't understand the prayer in tongues, because it does not originate in our mind but in our spirit. Our mind or understanding is unfruitful when we pray in tongues, but our spirit is very fruitful and edified, as we will see through our study.

Praying in the spirit in tongues is an exhilarating experience. In this type of prayer, there is a definite flow back and forth between the Holy Spirit and our spirit. The Holy Spirit gives us the utterance to speak words from our spirit, and we simply yield to Him and speak those words. In other words, praying in and with the Spirit is not one-way prayer where we generate all of the talking to God. It's a two-way type of prayer where we are listening to the Holy Spirit's prompting in our hearts and yielding to His leading and then verbalizing things to Him in our heavenly language.

To further build your faith and help you understand more about the subject of speaking and praying in tongues, let's look for common denominators on what happened when people in the Bible were filled with the Holy Spirit.

B. WHAT SHOULD WE EXPECT WHEN IT COMES TO PRAYING IN TONGUES?

To help establish this in your heart, let's look at every account in the book of Acts that describes believers being filled with the Spirit and ask what happened. What do these Scriptures say happened when the New Testament believers received the Holy Spirit? Can we prove that God's pattern in every account of believers being filled with the Spirit includes them speaking in tongues to pray, praise, and magnify the Lord? If so, that will give us great confirmation that as modern believers filled with the Spirit, God wants us to experience this great gift of being able to speak in tongues to pray, praise, and magnify Him as well.

1. Acts 2:4-11

And they were all filled with the Holy Spirit and began to speak with other tongues, as the Spirit gave them utterance. And there were dwelling in Jerusalem Jews, devout men, from every nation under heaven. And when this sound occurred, the multitude came together, and were confused, because everyone heard them speak in his own language. Then they were all amazed and marveled, saying to one another, "Look, are not all these who speak Galileans? And how *is it that* we hear, each in our own language in which we were born? Parthians and Medes and Elamites, those dwelling in Mesopotamia, Judea and Cappadocia, Pontus and Asia, Phrygia and Pamphylia, Egypt and the parts of Libya adjoining Cyrene, visitors from Rome, both Jews and proselytes, Cretans and Arabs—we hear them speaking in our own tongues the wonderful works of God."

When the early believers were filled with the Spirit, what was the first thing that happened? _____

Who enabled them to speak in tongues?_____

What languages did the Holy Spirit help them speak? _____

When people heard them speaking in tongues, what were they saying? _____

In this account, the believers were filled with the Spirit and spoke in tongues that were known languages. The languages were not known by the people speaking, but they were recognized by those who heard them.

2. Acts 9:1-18

Then Saul, still breathing threats and murder against the disciples of the Lord, went to the high priest and asked letters from him to the synagogues of Damascus, so that if he found any who were of the Way, whether men or women, he might bring them bound to Jerusalem. As he journeyed he came near Damascus, and suddenly a light shone around him from heaven. Then he fell to the ground, and heard a voice saying to him, "Saul, Saul, why are you persecuting Me?" And he said, "Who are You, Lord?" Then the Lord said, "I am Jesus, whom you are persecuting. It is hard for you to kick against the goads." So he, trembling and astonished, said, "Lord, what do You want me to do?" Then the Lord *said* to him, "Arise and go into the city, and you will be told what you must do." And the men who journeyed with him stood speechless, hearing a voice but seeing no one. Then Saul arose from the ground, and when his eyes were opened he saw no one. But they led him by the hand and brought *him* into Damascus. And he was three days without sight, and neither ate nor drank. Now there was a certain disciple at Damascus named Ananias; and to him the Lord said in a vision, "Ananias." And he said, "Here I am, Lord." So the Lord *said* to him, "Arise and go to the street called Straight, and inquire at the house of Judas for one called Saul of Tarsus, for behold, he is praying. And in a vision he has seen a man named Ananias coming in and putting *his* hand on him, so that he might receive his sight." Then Ananias answered, "Lord, I have heard from many about this man, how much harm he has done to Your saints in Jerusalem. And here he has authority from the chief priests to bind all who call on Your name." But the Lord said to him, "Go, for he is a chosen vessel of Mine to bear My name before Gentiles, kings, and the children of Israel. For I will show him how many things he must suffer for My name's sake." And Ananias went his way and entered the house; and laying his hands on him he said, "Brother Saul, the Lord Jesus, who appeared to you on the road as you came, has sent me that you may receive your sight and be filled with the Holy Spirit." Immediately there fell from his eyes *something* like scales, and he received his sight at once; and he arose and was baptized.

This is the dramatic account of Saul being born of the Spirit and subsequently being filled with the Spirit. Let's see what happened.

In verses 3-6, Saul who became the Apostle Paul had a dramatic conversion experience where he was born of the Spirit. What did he call Jesus in these verses? _____

In verses 17-18, God used Ananias to lay hands on Saul so he could receive and be filled with the Holy Spirit. What happened to Saul once he was filled with the Spirit? _____

We see scales falling from his eyes, but we don't see any evidence of Saul speaking in tongues in the account in Acts 9. But when we read Paul's letter to the Corinthians in 1 Corinthians 14:18-19, he tells us plainly, "I thank my God I speak with tongues more than you all; yet in the church I would rather speak five words with my understanding, that I may teach others also, than ten thousand words in a tongue."

According to 1 Corinthians 14:18-19, did the Apostle Paul (Saul) speak in tongues? _____

How often? _____

The Apostle Paul spoke in tongues privately more than anyone else!

3. Acts 10:44-46

While Peter was still speaking these words, the Holy Spirit fell upon all those who heard the word. And those of the circumcision who believed were astonished, as many as came with Peter, because the gift of the Holy Spirit had been poured out on the Gentiles also. For they heard them speak with tongues and magnify God.

What two things happened to these Gentile believers when they were filled with the Spirit? _____

4. Acts 19:6

And when Paul had laid hands on them, the Holy Spirit came upon them, and they spoke with tongues and prophesied.

When the Ephesian believers were filled with the Spirit, what happened to them? _____

5. Acts 8:5-21

Then Philip went down to the city of Samaria and preached Christ to them. And the multitudes with one accord heeded the things spoken by Philip, hearing and seeing the miracles which he did. For unclean spirits, crying with a loud voice, came out of many who were possessed; and many who were paralyzed and lame were healed. And there was great joy in that city. But there was a certain man called Simon, who previously practiced sorcery in the city and astonished the people of Samaria, claiming that he was someone great, to whom they all gave heed, from the least to the greatest, saying, "This man is the great power of God." And they heeded him because he had astonished them with his sorceries for a long time. But when they believed Philip as he preached the things concerning the kingdom of God and the name of Jesus Christ, both men and women were baptized. Then Simon himself also believed; and when he was baptized he continued with Philip, and was amazed, seeing the miracles and signs which were done. Now when the apostles who were at Jerusalem heard that Samaria had received the word of God, they sent Peter and John to them, who, when they had come down, prayed for them that they might receive the Holy Spirit. For as yet He had fallen upon none of them. They had only been baptized in the name of the Lord Jesus. Then they laid hands on them, and they received the Holy Spirit. And when Simon saw that through the laying on of the apostles' hands the Holy Spirit was given, he offered them money, saying, "Give me this power also, that anyone on whom I lay hands may receive the Holy Spirit." But Peter said to him, "Your money perish with you, because you thought that the gift of God could be purchased with money! You have neither part nor portion in this matter, for your heart is not right in the sight of God."

In this passage, it's not as obvious at first glance that the believers spoke in tongues when they were filled with the Spirit, but let's dig in and see what we can learn.

In verses 5, 12-14, what did Philip do? _____

How did the people respond to the gospel? _____

The people of Samaria heard the Gospel and believed the Word and were born of the Spirit.

In verses 14-17, what did Peter and John do? _____

What happened to the people? _____

In verse 18-19, Simon saw something he wanted to have the power to do. His heart was not right in his desire to obtain spiritual power, and he thought he could buy this power from the disciples.

What did Simon see that so intrigued him? _____

Simon's heart was not right with God and his motives were in the wrong place, but still, we can learn something from this passage and the way Simon responded. Simon saw something that got his attention. As a former sorcerer, he was not unaccustomed to seeing supernatural things, and as a person who followed Philip the evangelist, he saw many miracles and healings unfold right before his eyes, yet he never offered Philip money to have the power to heal people. So, what was it about seeing people being filled with the Spirit that got Simon's attention? He definitely saw something so unusual when the Samaritans were filled with the Spirit that he wanted this power. Based on the consistent record of the other accounts in the book of Acts where people were filled with the Spirit and spoke in tongues, we can easily conclude he saw them speaking in tongues. Our smoking gun comes from the clue we get in verse 21. Let's look at it.

In verses 20-21, Peter called Simon out and revealed his impure motives. Peter made an interesting statement when he said, "You have neither part nor portion in this *matter*, for your heart is not right in the sight of God."

When Peter said, "You have neither part nor portion in this matter," we find our clue. The word, "matter" is from the Greek word, *logos*. Logos is most often translated as a word, saying and speech in other places in the New Testament. The meanings for logos include "a word or saying, that which is spoken, also means an account which one gives by word of mouth"[1] So, we could read verse 21 this way: "You have neither part nor portion in this word, saying, speech, or that which is spoken. . . ."

In other words, Simon saw the Samaritans speaking words that caught his attention, so much so, that (although his motives were wrong) he wanted the supernatural power to reproduce this type of thing. It would be congruent with every other account of people being filled with the Spirit in the Book of Acts to read verse 21 like this: "You have neither part nor portion in this word of tongues. . . ."

Can you see from our study of looking at the accounts of believers who received the initial infilling of the Spirit in the book of Acts, that they all spoke in tongues? They may have also magnified God. They may have also prophesied, but the one common denominator in every account is that they spoke in tongues. That's great news for us, because the same thing still happens today. When you are filled with the Holy Spirit, you will have the supernatural ability to speak in other tongues to praise, pray, and magnify the Lord!

C. DIFFERENT KINDS OF TONGUES

Christians have espoused all kinds of crazy and comical things about speaking in tongues, and it's given the real expression of the Spirit a black eye. We've heard humorous stories about people being told they should say "keys to my Honda" over and over or "yabadabadoo" to prime the pump. That's what we call, cray-to-the-cray! If anyone ever tells you to do that, just say "sha-no-no!" The truth is, we don't manufacture or manipulate the ability to speak in tonugues, we simply yield to the Spirit and the words He gives us to speak.

Some people don't know what speaking tongues is, so they dismiss it completely. Others think that those who speak in tongues don't have control over themselves and go into some kind of a trance. There are those who think it's spooky and mystical. Still, others believe that speaking in tongues doesn't exist any longer. Again, let's look at what the Bible teaches.

The Bible describes varieties of tongues and shows us examples of people speaking in both the tongues of men and the tongues of angels. Sometimes, when a person speaks in tongues, it's in a recognized language. Someone on earth knows the language; although, the person speaking in tongues may not know the language. Sometimes when a person speaks in tongues, it's an unknown or unrecognized language, the tongues of angels. Again, it's not our job to figure out or manufacture speaking in tongues. Our job is to yield to the Spirit, and He will give us an utterance in tongues—either the tongues of men or angels. Let's look into the Scriptures and then fill in the blanks with what you see in the Word.

1. 1 Corinthians 13:1

Though I speak with the tongues of men and of angels, but have not love, I have become sounding brass or a clanging cymbal.

Tongues of _____ and of _____

2. 1 Corinthians 12:7-10

But the manifestation of the Spirit is given to each one for the profit of *all*: for to one is given the word of wisdom through the Spirit, to another the word of knowledge through the same Spirit, to another faith by the same Spirit, to another gifts of healings by the same Spirit, to another the working of miracles, to another prophecy, to another discerning of spirits, to another *different* kinds of tongues, to another the interpretation of tongues.

_____kinds of tongues

3. 1 Corinthians 12:28

And God has appointed these in the church: first apostles, second prophets, third teachers, after that miracles, then gifts of healings, helps, administrations, varieties of tongues.

_____of tongues

D. WHAT IS THE PURPOSE OF PRAYING IN TONGUES?

Many people have lumped all reasons for speaking in tongues together into one basket, but we can see from Scripture that there are at least two different purposes for speaking in tongues.

The first purpose for speaking in tongues that we can see in the Word of God is the public gift of tongues, which is used for ministry purposes in the local church or the assembly of believers. This gift of tongues is given when God desires to share a message of encouragement, comfort, or edification with a group of believers, and the message in tongues would require an interpretation. This might also be called the *public manifestation of tongues.* This manifestation is used, as the apostle Paul said, for ministry "in the church."

Another Biblical purpose for speaking in tongues is the private gift of tongues, which is used for personal prayer or edification. This might be called the *private manifestation of tongues* and does not necessarily require an interpretation. This manifestation is available for every believer, as the apostle Paul said, "to edify himself."

In the scriptures listed below, write the word "public" or "private" in the blank space to describe which manifestation of tongues the particular verse implies.

1. 1 Corinthians 12:28-30

And God has appointed these in the church: first apostles, second prophets, third teachers, after that miracles, then gifts of healings, helps, administrations, varieties of tongues. Are all apostles? Are all prophets? Are all teachers? Are all workers of miracles? Do all have gifts of healings? Do all speak with tongues? Do all interpret?

The keywords in this passage are "in the church."

---

2. 1 Corinthians 14:2

For he who speaks in a tongue does not speak to men but to God, for no one understands *him*; however, in the spirit he speaks mysteries.

The keywords in this verse are "to God."

___

3. 1 Corinthians 14:14,15

For if I pray in a tongue, my spirit prays, but my understanding is unfruitful. What is the conclusion then? I will pray with the spirit, and I will also pray with the understanding. I will sing with the spirit, and I will also sing with the understanding.

The keywords are "my spirit prays."

___

4. 1 Corinthians 14:26

How is it then, brethren? Whenever you come together, each of you has a psalm, has a teaching, has a tongue, has a revelation, has an interpretation. Let all things be done for edification.

The keywords are "whenever you come together."

___

5. 1 Corinthians 14:4

He who speaks in a tongue edifies himself, but he who prophesies edifies the church.

The keywords are "edifies himself."

___

6. 1 Corinthians 14:18-19

I thank my God I speak with tongues more than you all; yet in the church I would rather speak five words with my understanding, that I may teach others also, than ten thousand words in a tongue.

The key here is the contrast between verse 18 and verse 19.

Can you see the Scriptures teach both the public and private sides of speaking in tongues?

It is true that *not* everyone will have the public gift of speaking in tongues to convey a message. The public gift of tongues is given and directed as the Spirit desires.

It is true that *every* believer may have the private gift of speaking in tongues to pray or sing to the Lord. This is given by the Spirit to edify all believers who yield to Him. If you are a born–again, Spirit filled Christian and you have not yet spoken in tongues, this benefit is available to you today if you will simply yield to the Lord and allow yourself to speak or pray in the language He gives you. We'll describe this more throughout this chapter.

E. WHAT ARE THE BENEFITS OF PRAYING IN TONGUES?

There are numerous benefits to praying with the Spirit in tongues.

Here are a few:

- If you've wanted to be more effective in your witness for Christ and in having His boldness to live a Christ honoring life, praying in tongues builds and strengthens you on the inside.

- If you've ever wanted to praise the Lord from your innermost being and felt your natural language was inadequate, praising God in tongues is a great blessing.

- If you've ever wanted to thank God for all He has done for you but felt you didn't have an extensive enough vocabulary to do it justice, giving thanks in tongues brings a great deal of satisfaction.

- If you have ever wanted to talk to God heart to heart, but you couldn't seem to find the right words, speaking to the Lord in other tongues gives your heart a full expression.

- If you've ever wanted to pray about something but you just didn't know how to pray, the Holy Spirit will help you pray according to God's perfect will.

- If you've ever been in a demanding season or felt spiritually weary and needed to charge or recharge your inner man, praying in tongues along with spending extra time in God's Word will charge you up.

The Holy Spirit helps us talk to God from our heart of hearts through speaking in tongues.

As mentioned, speaking in tongues in our private lives is also called a prayer language or praying or speaking in the Spirit. When we exercise this prayer language, we literally bypass our mind and intellect, and we pray (or sing) straight from our spirit to God.

Speaking to God in our prayer language is like having a direct hotline to God, and our prayers and speech are not clouded by our thoughts, emotions, or feelings. As we pray in the Spirit, we receive a great spiritual blessing.

Are you tracking with all of this?

Some of you may be like me, you need things broken down and explained at a kindergarten level. I know I do. Many, many years ago after I was filled with the Spirit and our family was out fishing one day, I stared deep into the lake and pondered the life of a fish and this little parable was born. I hope it helps you see the benefits of speaking in tongues.

PARABLE OF THE FISH

Speaking in tongues is like a fish who lived in a lake . . .

A certain woman was out fishing one day and she had this thought,

"I wonder what goes through a fish's mind," she wondered, "when he bites into a worm, gets hooked and starts to travel at mach speed through the water, his eyes bugging out of his head, (which apparently they do all the time) and his dorsal fin at attention on threat level five?"

She imagined the whole scene.

Before the fish can say goodbye to his family and friends, he's yanked through the water with his lip half ripped off, screaming *"Whoaaa!"* The next thing he knows, he's flying through the air with the greatest of ease—that is, before he bangs up against a boat. He must wonder if he's been abducted by aliens or is tripping on some bad weeds.

It doesn't take him long to realize he's not in Kansas any longer, no water on his scales, no weeds, minnows or clams to harass. Once inside the boat, before he has a chance to catch his breath, someone without any manners puts him in a straightjacket grip and starts to give him what feels like a root canal or lip injections. He thinks he's going to die a terrible death, when suddenly this mannerless person jerks one last time. The fish feels excruciating pain and then instant relief as a hook is ripped from his lip!

As he looks around he realizes this kingdom is completely different. Much brighter than the lake and oh, so huge! And these beings, humans, they speak in a strange tongue. His only language is "fish speak." If only he could talk in the human tongue, he might say, "I come in peace. My fish mean no harm. Release the death grip," or something like that.

The next thing he knows, a young human is talking to him. "What did you do, skip school? Ha-ha, get it? School? School of fish?" No response from the fish. That didn't stop the human. "You should have listened to your parents and not talked to, or uh, eaten strange worms!" (The human is doing a whole stand up routine, yet the fish never blinks.)

An older human must have felt some compassion as he tells the fish, "It's ok, little buddy. Everything is going to be fine. Don't worry; I am going to put you back in the lake. When you go back, tell all your friends, 'Don't eat worms!' That'll save your life! I have many other things to say to you, but you are not able to bear them now." The fish nods in compliance, not because he understands, but to save his scales.

Once back in the lake, the fish swims away like a bat out of you know where and thinks to himself, "No one will ever believe this." He rehearses his explanation, "Hey family, friends, guys, I uh, well, uh, I had an out-of-lake experience. There's another kingdom beyond the surface of the water! No, I didn't 'see a bright light' or a 'stairway.' Don't laugh! I'm not kidding. The humans exist! I was there. I heard them. They talked to me. Hey, ya'll ever heard of speaking in human tongues? If we could just learn their language . . . it could be a game changer. No, I didn't hit my head. It's not a cult. No, I wasn't in a trance. I didn't smoke the weeds. Seriously, c'mon, does anyone believe me?"

After this imaginary parable went through the woman's head, she thought, "Wouldn't it be great if the fish could talk to and learn from the human? After all, the fish only knows what he can see, taste, and touch in his own lake. Little does he know how massive the kingdom of the human really is and how many other lakes, rivers, and streams, not to mention oceans, mountains, valleys, and deserts there are. The human could tell him so many things that would protect him, help him and lengthen his life, if only he could speak a little human!"

Let him who has ears to hear . . . hear.

It's a simple little story, but the truth is, we're a lot like the fish!

Obviously, God (as represented by the human in this parable) and His kingdom are so beyond our human understanding. As humans (repped by the fish), our knowledge base, reference points, and our human language are so limited. If only we could speak in God's language (tongues!), the quality of our communication and interpretation of God and His kingdom could be so enhanced.

Did you follow all that? (I know. Theologians are now rolling over in their graves.) It's not a perfect illustration, but there are some parallels.

God has not only given us the ability to communicate with Him in our everyday language, but He's also given us the ability and supernatural advantage of being able to communicate with Him in His language, the heavenly language of speaking in tongues. And what a blessing that is!

Let's look at the benefits of praying or singing in tongues.

1. 1 Corinthians 14:2

For he who speaks in a tongue does not speak to men but to God, for no one understands him; however, in the spirit he speaks mysteries.

Who are we speaking to when we pray in tongues? _____

_____

What are we speaking? _____

_____

When we speak to God in tongues, we can pray things that may be a mystery to us, but they are not mysteries to God. For example, most everything about our future, our calling, who we will marry, where we will live, the children we will have and so much more, is all a big mystery to us. When we pray in tongues, the Holy Spirit will help us pray things related to our future. A minister friend of ours once said, "When we pray in the Spirit, we pray out the future track we will run on."

2. 1 Corinthians 14:4

He who speaks in a tongue edifies himself, but he who prophesies edifies the church.

What happens to someone who prays in tongues? _____ _____

_____

Edify: This means "to charge up.[2]" Just like charging up a battery, our spirit will be charged or built up with strength and power as we pray in tongues.

When you feel like your spiritual battery needs to be recharged, praying or singing in tongues is one of the most effective ways to charge your spirit. You will sense the Lord's presence and His power filling your inner man.

3. Jude 20

But you, beloved, building yourselves up on your most holy faith, praying in the Holy Spirit,

97

How do we build ourselves up on our most holy faith? _____

Praying in the Holy Spirit: One of the best habits you can get into early in your Christian life, is praying in the Holy Spirit. When you pray in tongues, not as a mindless exercise but with the awareness that you pray in tongues, you are literally charging up your spirit and building yourself up on your most holy faith.

I hope you are catching on to the importance and power of praying in tongues in your private life on a regular basis. This dedicated time of worship and praying in the Spirit is between you and the Lord. At times, you may be tempted to avoid praying in tongues because your mind does not always understand or have the full interpretation of what you are praying about, but if you will determine to pray in tongues as you go throughout your day, whether you understand what you are praying or not, you will find yourself enjoying an intimate friendship with the Holy Spirit, being built up from the inside out.

4. Romans 8:26-28

Likewise the Spirit also helps in our weaknesses. For we do not know what we should pray for as we ought, but the Spirit Himself makes intercession for us with groanings which cannot be uttered. Now He who searches the hearts knows what the mind of the Spirit *is*, because He makes intercession for the saints according to the *will of* God. And we know that all things work together for good to those who love God, to those who are the called according to *His* purpose.

When will the Holy Spirit help us? _____

Have you ever needed to pray about something, but you didn't know how to pray? _____

How will the Holy Spirit help us? _____

_____

I remember a season in my life when I was single and wanted nothing more than to meet the man of my dreams and get married—and fulfill the calling I sensed on my life for ministry. I didn't know how all of those desires were going to come together and I didn't know how to pray about it! I had graduated from Boston University with a degree in communications, and I was in Bible School preparing for ministry. I wasn't dating anyone, and I had been disappointed by a few previous relationships. To top off the "dating disillusionment trifecta," there was no single, available hunk on the horizon! I had prayed, begged, waited, cried and prayed some more, but it felt like a dating famine had hit my life. I certainly couldn't manufacture Prince Charming, and by this time, I had thrown away my "20 Things I Want in a Husband" list and had boiled it down to this:

"3 Things I Would Settle For—Christian. Tall. Breathing."

I definitely felt like I had a weakness. I didn't know how to pray about marriage or ministry. My only hope was getting the Holy Spirit's help! I knew He would help me pray it out as I prayed in the Spirit. I knew He would help me pray according to God's perfect will and that in the end, all things would work together for my good because I loved the Lord and I was called according to His purpose.

So, I dedicated the time I spent driving in my car to prayer. I told the Lord that whenever I got in my car to go to work, I would begin praying in the Spirit, and I would trust the Holy Spirit to help me pray according to His perfect will concerning my future marriage and ministry. Every time I got in my car and began driving, I would get quiet on the inside and ask the Lord to help me pray. Then, I began to pray in tongues and groanings from my heart of hearts. (Trust me, the groanings part was easy to come by. I so desired to "give birth" to the man of my dreams, it was easy to yield to the Spirit in prayer this way.) I could sense the Holy Spirit making intercession through me.

This went on for about two weeks. One day, I had been praying in the Spirit while driving and about halfway along on my drive while stopped at a light, I sensed the desire to laugh rather than pray in tongues. So, I started laughing in my car while sitting at the red light! (I probably looked like some freakazoid to those in the cars next to me as I laughed all by myself during the red light!) When the light turned green, I started driving again and had an *aha!* moment, as I realized that I had literally "prayed out" God's will for the next season of my life in marriage and ministry. I felt such joy and a "knowing" that I had prayed according to God's perfect will concerning marriage and ministry as described in Romans 8:26-27, and now I knew that Romans 8:28 belonged to me. I knew "that all things work together for good to those who love God, to those who are the called according to His purpose."

I am happy to report that within the next three months, the Lord answered my prayers. I met my husband Jeff! (And for the record, he is exceedingly, abundantly above and beyond tall, Christian, and breathing!) We were married one year later in 1986. Then, we moved to Oklahoma to start our marriage and study for the ministry. Three years later, the Lord led us to move back home to Michigan to start a church. Now, over thirty years, four kids and a growing church later, I look back and marvel at all the supernatural things that the Lord has done. I am convinced that dedicating those few weeks to praying in the Spirit helped me to "pray out a part of the track we would run on" in a very important season of our lives.

Do you have a deep-seated desire in your heart, and you just don't know how to pray about it? Are you experiencing a weakness where you just don't know what to do or how to pray? I encourage you to dedicate some time to praying in tongues about it. The Holy Spirit will help you just as He did me.

5. Ephesians 6:10-20

Finally, my brethren, be strong in the Lord and in the power of His might. Put on the whole armor of God, that you may be able to stand against the wiles of the devil. For we do not wrestle against flesh and blood, but against principalities, against powers, against the rulers of the darkness of this age, against spiritual hosts of wickedness in the heavenly places. Therefore take up the whole armor of God, that you may be able to withstand in the evil day, and having done all, to stand. Stand therefore, having girded your waist with truth, having put on the breastplate of righteousness, and having shod your feet with the preparation of the gospel of peace; above all, taking the shield of faith with which you will be able to quench all the fiery darts of the wicked one. And take the helmet of salvation, and the sword of the Spirit, which is the word of God; praying always with all prayer and supplication in the Spirit, being watchful to this end with all perseverance and supplication for all the saints—and for me, that utterance may be given to me, that I may open my mouth boldly to make known the mystery of the gospel, for which I am an ambassador in chains; that in it I may speak boldly, as I ought to speak.

According to verse 18, how should we pray? _____

What do the phrases "in the Spirit" and "being watchful" mean to you? _____

What does this passage on the spiritual armor reveal to us about prayer? _____

What and who are we to pray for? _____

6. 1 Corinthians 14:12-19

Even so you, since you are zealous for spiritual *gifts, let it be* for the edification of the church *that* you seek to excel. Therefore let him who speaks in a tongue pray that he may interpret. For if I pray in a tongue, my spirit prays, but my understanding is unfruitful. What is *the conclusion* then? I will pray with the spirit, and I will also pray with the understanding. I will sing with the spirit, and I will also sing with the understanding. Otherwise, if you bless with the spirit, how will he who occupies the place of the uninformed say "Amen" at your giving of thanks, since he does not understand what you say? For you indeed give thanks well, but the other is not edified. I thank my God I speak with tongues more than you all; yet in the church I would rather speak five words with my understanding, that I may teach others also, than ten thousand words in a tongue.

When it comes to speaking and praying in tongues, we are encouraged to always keep the best interests of others in mind. Notice, in our private lives we ought to pray in the Spirit often, but in the church we ought to speak words that those listening can either interpret or understand.

What do we learn from verse 12? _____

According to verse 14-15, what are two ways you can pray? _____

_____

According to verse 13, what should you pray to do? _____

_____

According to verses 16-17, how can we give thanks? _____

_____

According to verse 18, what did the Apostle Paul do more than anyone else? _____

Ever thought about the connection between Paul's admission of speaking in tongues (in his private life) more than anyone else in Corinth and his being the one God used to write over half of the New Testament? When we pray in tongues, the Holy Spirit gives us revelation and God's Word comes alive. Perhaps as he prayed in tongues, the Spirit gave him revelation and God's Word (at least his portion of the New Testament) came into existence!

When we develop a regular, private prayer life, it becomes evident outside of our prayer closet. We can and should pray in our known language with our minds and understanding, and we can and should pray in tongues from our spirit.

F. PRAYING, SINGING AND BEING FULL OF THE SPIRIT IS FUN!

The Bible uses fun metaphors for being filled with the Spirit and for praying and singing in tongues. Let's look at how being filled with the Spirit is compared and contrasted to being drunk with wine.

1. Acts 2:4-21

The second chapter of Acts describes a fun scene, people speaking in tongues and having such joy that the onlookers thought they were drunk. Sounds like a good time to me—joy, intoxicated with the Spirit, and acting like a happy drunk, with no hangover! Let's look at it.

> And they were all filled with the Holy Spirit and began to speak with other tongues, as the Spirit gave them utterance. And there were dwelling in Jerusalem Jews, devout men, from every nation under heaven. And when this sound occurred, the multitude came together, and were confused, because everyone heard them speak in his own language. Then they were all amazed and marveled, saying to one another, "Look, are not all these who speak Galileans? And how *is it that* we hear, each in our own language in which we were born? Parthians and Medes and Elamites, those dwelling in Mesopotamia, Judea and Cappadocia, Pontus and Asia, Phrygia and Pamphylia, Egypt and the parts of Libya adjoining Cyrene, visitors from Rome, both Jews and proselytes, Cretans and Arabs—we hear them speaking in our own tongues the wonderful works of God." So they were all amazed and perplexed, saying to one another, "Whatever could this mean?" Others mocking said, "They are full of new wine." But Peter, standing up with the eleven, raised his voice and said to them, "Men of Judea and all who dwell in Jerusalem, let this be known to you, and heed my words. For these are not drunk, as you suppose, since it is only the third hour of the day. But this is what was spoken by the prophet Joel:
>
> > 'And it shall come to pass in the last days, says God,
> > That I will pour out of My Spirit on all flesh;
> > Your sons and your daughters shall prophesy,
> > Your young men shall see visions,
> > Your old men shall dream dreams.
> > And on My menservants and on My maidservants

I will pour out My Spirit in those days;
And they shall prophesy.
I will show wonders in heaven above
And signs in the earth beneath:
Blood and fire and vapor of smoke.
The sun shall be turned into darkness,
And the moon into blood,
Before the coming of the great and awesome day of
    the LORD.
And it shall come to pass
That whoever calls on the name of the LORD
Shall be saved.'"

What happened in verse 4? _____

In verses 6-11, what happened to those who were filled with the Spirit? _____ _____

In verses 12-15, the believers were filled with joy and freedom and the ability to praise God in a heavenly language. Their behavior caused those observing to mock and accuse them of being what? _____

_____

In verses 16-21, how did Peter describe this experience? _____

_____

2. Ephesians 5:18-20, NLT

Don't be drunk with wine, because that will ruin your life. Instead, be filled with the Holy Spirit, singing psalms and hymns and spiritual songs among yourselves, and making music to the Lord in your hearts. And give thanks for everything to God the Father in the name of our Lord Jesus Christ.

When we are filled with the Spirit, what will it cause us to do? __

_____

When you think about singing and making music to the Lord, does that sound scary or boring? _____

_____

Often, people get drunk with wine (or other types of alcohol) because they believe it's fun—temporarily. Getting intoxicated or under the influence of alcohol allows people to laugh, to make up songs, to converse and forget their problems. Being tipsy or drunk causes people to forget their inhibitions and fears and they say, sing, and do things they would never do or say when sober. Often, they do and say things they regret. The Lord doesn't want us to get drunk because it's not all fun and games. In fact, it can be very damaging and deadly and is a counterfeit to what He offers.

There is a real experience of being *drunk* and *under the influence of the Spirit* where you are refreshed, strengthened, and empowered. We can be filled with the Spirit and enjoy His joy, laughter, and the ability to make up songs and melodies to the Lord. Being intoxicated with the Spirit helps us to overcome our self-conscious inhibitions and fears. When you think about it, staying filled with the Spirit and under His influence is something we should desire and practice every day!

How would you describe being intoxicated or under the influence of the Spirit, not wine? _____

Have you ever received a Spirit–inspired psalm, hymn, or spiritual song? _____

Can you share it? _____

We can sing psalms, hymns, and spiritual songs to the Lord in both our everyday language and in tongues.

Personally, I enjoy singing in the Spirit and then singing the words in English afterwards. Often, the words I sing in English are the interpretation of what I've sung in tongues. Some of the songs I've gotten from the Lord over the years have really encouraged me and charged up my spirit with strength. Perhaps a few of the songs I received will encourage you and prime the pump so you sing your own songs and melodies to the Lord.

The Other Way Around – 1999

I was the one who thought that I found You,
But You were the One, and I was found by You.
I was the one who thought that I sought Your face,
But You were the One who sought me in the first place.

I was the one who thought that I loved You,
But You were the One, that gave Your life, my Redeemer, true.

All along, it was the other way around . . .
You are the One, I now do see,
You loved me first and reached out to me.
I was the one, that You had in mind,
When You laid down Your life, on the cross divine.
You are the One that I worship and adore
And I am the one that longs for You more and more.

Stepping Out – 2000

Stepping out in the things of God,
I'm reminded to do,
To flow from my heart in fellowship with You.

Speaking phrases and words that come to heart and mind,
I'm singing and writing things divine.

They bless, refresh, and strengthen my soul.
Spending time in this daily has become my goal.
Where the river flows it brings fresh life,
Reviving my spirit. I feel so alive!

Fresh manna from heaven, daily from You
Speaking psalms, hymns, and spiritual songs
I know what to do.
Yielding, yielding, and speaking by faith.
Simply yielding and yielding, You give me great grace.

God Has a Word for the Weary – 2007
God has a word for the weary; God has a word for the weak;
God has a word for the weary, and His word is simply *speak*!

Don't be silent. Don't be silent.
Don't doubt. Don't pout.
Don't be silent. Don't you doubt, and don't you pout.
But let the weak speak—let the weak speak,
Let the weak say, "I am strong."
God is not wrong.

Let the weak and the weary, let them not become bleary.
But let them speak and sing the Word.
Sing the Word, sing the Word . . . declare what you know
And you'll find God is with you from your heart as you go.
Sing it out. Sing it out. Sing it loud. Sing it strong.

You may not even know what to say, but that's okay
The words will come. Just speak and sing it now.
God has a word for the weary, and God has a word for the weak
And this is His word are you listening?
His word to you is *speak*!

G. HOW DO WE YIELD TO AND PRAY WITH THE HOLY SPIRIT?

If you have asked the Lord to fill you with the Spirit, and you have not yet experienced this wonderful flow of speaking and praying in the Spirit in other tongues, it's not hard. Really, it's the simplest thing in the world to do. You just simply yield to the Holy Spirit and start speaking. (The keyword is: yield!)

You might wonder, how do you yield to the Spirit in tongues? To yield is a rest, not a striving. To yield, don't try to initiate a thought in your head, just listen to the words or phrases the Holy Spirit is giving you on the inside—within your heart—and then utter them and say them out loud.

As you yield to the Spirit, you will speak in tongues. The Holy Spirit doesn't speak in tongues, but He will give you the utterance, and you will do the speaking. As you begin to move your mouth and vocal chords, you will sense a river of living water coming up from your innermost being. As you yield, the Holy Spirit will give you the words and you will flow in this spiritual language.

We receive the Spirit by faith. We speak in other tongues as we yield to the Holy Spirit.

You might wonder, what if you don't feel anything? What if you don't feel a river bubbling up on the inside of you? Remember, feelings have nothing to do with Bible facts. If you have asked God to fill you with the Spirit, then believe He has done exactly that. Expect the evidence of speaking in tongues as the Scriptures teach. As you worship God, you will find the river in your spirit rising. Your English vocabulary will be inadequate and as you yield to the Lord, you will find yourself speaking words you have never learned.

Sometimes, when people lean towards trying to understand everything about being filled with the Spirit from an analytical or logical angle, they don't feel anything at all and they get stuck. I know from experience! The best thing to do is to get out of your head and get flowing with the Lord from your heart. Don't overthink it. Just flow from your heart, and you will enter a new threshold in your relationship with the Lord and your experience with the Holy Spirit and His power.

Ultimately, we are not led by feelings; we are led by faith in God, His Word and His promises. As you learn to yield to the Holy Spirit, you will find the flow, and your ability to yield to Him will come more easily.

Learning about being filled with the Spirit and yielding to Him to speak in other tongues is such a wonderful time between you and the Lord. Remember, He is your guide, and He will lead you all the way. To help you in your experience with the Spirit, here are a few helpful hints:

- Remember, God wants this for you. It is His will that you enjoy the fullness of being filled with the Spirit and speaking and praying in tongues. The private manifestation of speaking in tongues is for you and all believers who are filled with the Spirit. Your heart will have such a freedom of expression as you pray in the Spirit.

- Speak out the words He gives you. You may sense the desire to speak a fluent language or just one or two words that are foreign to you. Don't wait for an entire language; just speak out the one or two words you receive. As you speak them out in faith, more will come.

- Spend extended time in worship. Quiet your mind and focus on the Lord. Begin to magnify God in your everyday language. When you run out of words in your language, you'll be primed and ready to continue worshipping Him. Yielding in tongues will come easily.

- Set aside time to sing and worship the Lord. One person I know said it was easier for them to yield to the Spirit and speak in tongues as they were singing. They started by singing along to a worship song on the radio, and as they sang the melody, their spirit began to sing in tongues and magnify the Lord.

- Pray for things your heart really cares about. I know a woman who was filled with the Spirit by faith, but she had a hard time yielding to Him to pray in her heavenly prayer language. She was being analytical and trying to speak in tongues from her head instead of her heart. One day, she was asked to pray for a family that she dearly loved. It was easy for her to pray from her heart for them, and when she started to pray for them in her everyday language, she instantly yielded to the Spirit and started to pray for them in tongues.

- Focus on the Giver, not on the gift of praying in tongues. Sometimes people get so focused on praying in tongues, they forget to keep their focus on the Giver, God himself. As a result, they try too hard to manufacture something. Praying in tongues is not something we manufacture from our head; it's a gift from the Lord that comes out of our heart. Just relax and focus on Him.

If you find yourself struggling to yield or your logical, analytical mind keeps having legitimate questions that bounce around in your head, be patient. You'll get there. You are not alone. Let's answer some of the common questions people have about this topic.

H. 10 COMMON QUESTIONS AND MISUNDERSTANDINGS ABOUT SPEAKING AND PRAYING IN TONGUES

In this chapter, we have briefly touched on the public gift of tongues, but our primary focus has been on the private gift of tongues in our prayer lives. People often have questions when it comes to both the public gift of tongues and the private ability to pray in tongues, so let's look at some of the common questions and misunderstandings that often arise.

1. Is it true that not everyone has the gift of tongues?

It is true that not everyone has the *public* gift of tongues for ministry in a congregation or church setting. The public operation of the gift of tongues is given as the Spirit desires, and not everyone has this gift.

However, this is not true concerning the *private* manifestation of tongues for prayer and personal, spiritual edification. The private manifestation of tongues is available to every believer, as seen in 1 Corinthians 14:5 where the Apostle Paul says he would desire for all of us to speak in tongues.

It is clear that Paul is advocating the private use of tongues for personal edification as he had explained in verse 4. However, in the church (in public) he would rather have us prophesy or speak in tongues with the interpretation so that the inspired utterances can be understood by all.

2. I was told that when a person speaks in tongues, someone should always interpret what was spoken. Is that true?

Good question. I think the answer is yes and no. That's because it depends upon whether you are talking about the public or private gift of tongues. Here's why.

We know God does not give everyone the public gift of tongues, but when He chooses to give this gift to someone and they bring forth a public message in tongues, the answer is yes, it requires an interpretation. That's because the Holy Spirit wants to communicate a message to a group of believers through the operation of the public gift of tongues, and this does require an interpretation. First Corinthians 14:26 says, "How is it then, brethren? Whenever you come together, each of you has a psalm, has a teaching, has a tongue, has a revelation, has an interpretation. Let all things be done for edification. If anyone speaks in a tongue, let there be two or at the most three, each in turn, and let one interpret. But if there is no interpreter, let him keep silent in church, and let him speak to himself and to God."

You can see this is a reference to a public setting, "when you come together." The person who gives a public message in tongues might be the one to interpret it also, or another person in the meeting may be given the interpretation. Note that an interpretation is not a translation. Sometimes a person may give a public message in tongues which is very short—let's say 20 or 30 seconds. The person giving the interpretation might take three minutes to give the interpretation. That's because they are not translating word for word, but are interpreting what the Holy Spirit wants that group of people to receive in the message He inspired in tongues. When it comes to a public setting (like a believers meeting, church service or prayer meeting) keep in mind that everything should be done decently and in order and with the blessing of the God-appointed leader of that meeting (the pastor, leader, etc.).

When it comes to the private gift of speaking in tongues for the purposes of prayer and building up your own spirit, the answer is no, interpretation is not required. That's because the Holy Spirit is not necessarily giving a message to a group of believers; rather, He has given believers the ability to pray in tongues. Praying is different from a speaking a public message.

3. Is there any scriptural basis for praying or singing in tongues?

Yes! As we have seen in 1 Corinthians 14:14-15 (KJV), the Apostle Paul said he could "pray in an unknown tongue." The ability to pray in tongues is also called "praying in the Spirit," or praying in a "prayer language." Praying in unknown tongues is distinct from speaking in tongues with an interpretation. Praying in tongues is just that—it's prayer and it's scriptural. Praying in tongues is something that is done privately or in a group prayer setting, and this is different than giving a public utterance in tongues with an interpretation.

I remember the first time I saw people praying and singing in the Spirit. I was in a church service and I along with many others were following the worship leader and singing worship songs in English—our everyday language. I looked around the room and noticed that many people near me had their eyes closed, but their lips were moving. They weren't singing the same words I was singing. I caught just a little bit of what those nearby were saying, and they were singing in what sounded like a foreign language. It was quite beautiful. It was so melodic and seemed to just flow from their hearts right to the Lord.

In 1 Corinthians 14, Paul explains that while he was praying in the Spirit, his spirit prayed and his understanding was unfruitful. When he prayed in the Spirit or in other tongues, it came from his spirit and his mind did not understand what he was saying. Notice, he also included the personal benefit of singing in the Spirit. To pray and sing in the Spirit (in other tongues) for personal edification is, indeed, scriptural. It is important to mention that, according to 1 Corinthians 14:2, when we pray or speak in unknown tongues privately, we are speaking to

God, not to men and not to the devil. When we speak in our prayer language, we are speaking out mysteries and edifying ourselves.

Again, the ability to pray in tongues is distinctly different from being prompted by the Spirit to give a public message in tongues, which requires an interpretation. The Holy Spirit gives the public gift of tongues along with the interpretation so that those who hear it are encouraged, comforted, and edified.

4. Our church doesn't believe in speaking in tongues, and I was taught tongues have passed away and are no longer in use. Is this true?

It is good to respect your church's beliefs and doctrines. However, if your church's beliefs and doctrines ever conflict with the written Word of God, then you need to take sides with the Word of God. Jesus referred to believers speaking in tongues when He gave the Great Commission to the Church in Mark 16:17. In 1 Corinthians 14:39 Paul said, "Forbid not to speak with tongues."

Some churches and entire denominations teach a cessation theology based in part upon 1 Corinthians 13:8-10: "But whether there are prophecies, they will fail; whether there are tongues, they will cease; whether there is knowledge, it will vanish away. For we know in part and we prophesy in part. But when that which is perfect has come, then that which is in part will be done away." In essence, this teaching postulates that when the disciples passed away and when the New Testament was written, the perfect came and tongues ceased. If that which is perfect has come and tongues have ceased, then, according to this particular passage of Scripture, prophecy and knowledge also would have ceased. We know, however, that knowledge has not ceased; but, in fact, it has actually increased. Therefore, it seems that the perfect has not come, yet. The perfect shall come when He, the perfect One, appears in His Second Coming. Until that time comes, tongues, prophecy, and knowledge are still with us.

5. I don't want anything spooky or over-the-top. How do I know this is real and from God?

I understand. Seems like our human tendency is to go to extremes. We run away from things we fear, don't value, or don't understand or we go overboard on things we love (like getting every piece of equipment plus new shoes, new spandex and a headband when we think we might want to start working out). When it comes to being filled with the Spirit, it seems like we do the same thing. We either shrink back and run away from Him, or we go overboard and run past Him with extreme behavior.

God is not spooky. God doesn't do things to embarrass people. The ability to pray in tongues and flow with the Spirit is a wonderful supernatural blessing.

The best way to know if something is real and from God is to be sure it is congruent with His Word. That's why we are spending so much time studying the Word to learn what God has said about this topic. We are told to "judge" spiritual things with God's Word as our standard. Here are a few scriptures that will help you to discern the authentic work of the Holy Spirit.

You can be at peace and trust the Lord. First Corinthians 14 tells us, "For God is not the author of confusion but of peace."

Romans 14:17 tells us, "for the kingdom of God is not eating and drinking, but righteousness and peace and joy in the Holy Spirit." He always leads to righteousness, peace, and joy!

Second Corinthians 3:17 says, "Now the Lord is the Spirit; and where the Spirit of the Lord *is*, there *is* liberty."

His gifts and intentions towards us are always for our good. Surely He wants every believer to experience the normal yet very supernatural Spirit–empowered life.

6. Will the Holy Spirit take over my mouth? I'm afraid if I speak in tongues, it will get out of control.

No. The Holy Spirit will not take over your mouth. Acts 2:4 says, "they were all filled with the Holy Spirit and began to speak with other tongues, as the Spirit gave them utterance." You will do the speaking. The Holy Spirit will give you the utterance, but you control your own mouth and vocal chords. The Holy Spirit doesn't speak in tongues; you will do the speaking. In other words, you may feel a sensation in your vocal chords or you may feel like expressing certain words or you may have a sense of wanting to talk in words that sound like baby talk, but you do the speaking. At first, there may seem to be one or two words or maybe a whole sentence just bubbling up from within you. When you simply yield to that, you will flow in speaking in tongues.

Keep in mind, you will be in control of yielding to the Spirit. He fills you and gives you the utterance, but you have a free will and the ability to turn it on and off, so to speak.

Think about being filled with the Spirit and speaking in tongues like the plumbing system in your home. Once your pipes are filled with water, you are in control of turning the faucet on or off to let the water flow through the pipes and out through a faucet. In the same way, once you ask the Lord to fill you with His Spirit, the rivers of living water are in the pipes, so to speak. You are in control of turning the faucet on or off by opening or closing your mouth and allowing the rivers of living water to flow through in a heavenly language of tongues.

You will never speak in tongues out of control. This is a common fear. Don't worry, you won't be at work or walking through the grocery store and then suddenly burst out in tongues at some inopportune time. Paul clearly says in 1 Corinthians 14:32 that the spirits of the prophets are subject to the prophets. In other words, you have control over your spirit and mouth. God never forces anyone to do anything. He will never embarrass you by causing you to speak in tongues beyond your control. A person can always control their ability to yield to the Lord in the starting and stopping of speaking or praying in tongues. God will never violate your free will.

7. I am afraid a demon might speak through me instead of the Holy Spirit. Will this happen?

This is a common fear. Perhaps the devil uses this thought to keep people from speaking in tongues because he himself fears the power of God released through people who speak in tongues. You can be comforted to know that you will receive a good gift from God, not a demon.

I understand this fear; I was one of those who had been taught against the subject of speaking in tongues, so I held on to my fearful position. I was like a kid holding onto my lunchbox full of fears, not realizing that God wanted me to let go of my lunchbox and exchange it for a giant buffet!

You can trust Jesus. In Luke 11:9-13, He assures us that if we ask the Father for the Holy Spirit, He will not give us something else. Let's read this passage and see God's goodness:

> "So I say to you, ask, and it will be given to you; seek, and you will find; knock, and it will be opened to you. For everyone who

asks receives, and he who seeks finds, and to him who knocks it will be opened. If a son asks for bread from any father among you, will he give him a stone? Or if he asks for a fish, will he give him a serpent instead of a fish? Or if he asks for an egg, will he offer him a scorpion? If you then, being evil, know how to give good gifts to your children, how much more will your heavenly Father give the Holy Spirit to those who ask Him!"

8. Does someone have to pray and lay hands on me in order for me to receive the gift of speaking in tongues?

Not necessarily. There are different ways to receive the Holy Spirit. The main element to receiving the Holy Spirit is to simply ask and believe. However, there is a scriptural precedent for receiving the Holy Spirit by the laying on of hands. Some people find it helpful to have hands laid upon them as a point of contact to release their faith to receive and yield to the Holy Spirit, but it is not an absolute for all believers. There is scriptural precedent for receiving the Spirit, hearing the Word of God and receiving. There is also scriptural precedent for asking God and receiving without the laying on of hands. So, as you can see there are many methods for ministering and receiving the Spirit. The most important thing is to believe and receive the Holy Spirit by faith, then yield to the Spirit to pray in the heavenly language He gives.

On the Day of Pentecost over 2000 years ago, Jesus sent the Holy Spirit to the Church. He is here, and we can simply receive Him by faith.

9. I have non-Christian friends who seem to be freaked out by the subject of speaking in tongues. Does the Bible say tongues are a sign for them?

You are referring to 1 Corinthians 14:22-25: "Therefore tongues are for a sign, not to those who believe but to unbelievers; but prophesying is not for unbelievers but for those who believe. Therefore if the whole church comes together in one place, and all speak with tongues, and there come in those who are uninformed or unbelievers, will they not say that you are out of your mind? But if all prophesy, and an unbeliever or an uninformed person comes in, he is convinced by all, he is convicted by all. And thus the secrets of his heart are revealed; and so, falling down on his face, he will worship God and report that God is truly among you."

Theologians and Bible scholars have various views on this passage. I like what commentator David Guzik said, "Perhaps, Paul is saying something like this: 'A good principle of understanding the Bible is always to interpret what is hard to understand in light of what is easier to understand. First Corinthians 14:23-25 seem easier to understand, because it is easy to see how an unbeliever hearing Christians speaking in tongues might say that you are out of your mind. It is also easy to see that prophecy could convict the heart of an unbeliever, causing them to repent, and to worship God and report that God is truly among you. So, while we may not exactly understand what Paul means by tongues are a sign, not to those who believe but to unbelievers, we know he does not mean tongues "minister" to or edify unbelievers. Tongues do nothing to bring an unbeliever closer to God; they may instead turn him off.'"[3]

He went on to say, "If you insist on speaking in tongues in your church meetings, instead of in your own personal devotional life, the only good that comes from that use of tongues is that is a sign of judgment to unbelievers. Because they think you are crazy when they hear you speaking so, it simply shows they don't understand the things of God and are headed towards judgment. But how much better if you were to emphasize prophecy instead of tongues, then everyone could be blessed, believer and unbeliever together!"[4]

In summary, 1 Corinthians 2:14 gives us some insights, "But the natural man does not receive the things of the Spirit of God, for they are foolishness to him; nor can he know *them,* because they are spiritually discerned." It is our understanding that as believers, we can and should pray in tongues privately or with other believers as often as we desire. When it comes to speaking in tongues publicly, our experience has been that when unbelievers (natural men) are present, they don't understand speaking in tongues or the things of the Spirit and it will seem like foolishness to them.

10. Speaking in tongues seems so silly. Is it really beneficial?

To our natural mind, speaking in tongues may seem silly. After all, the idea that from our spirits we could speak in a heavenly language we don't know, don't understand, and have never learned does seem a little strange! Our minds naturally want to know and understand everything. However, we have to remember that God is a Spirit not a mind, and sometimes while our minds will not comprehend every spiritual thing, our inner man will have an assurance that speaking in tongues is a true and genuine gift from the Lord. Perhaps that is why Paul said in 1 Corinthians 1:27, "But God hath chosen the foolish things of the world to confound the wise; and God hath chosen the weak things of the world to confound the things which are mighty."

We've covered a lot in this chapter! I hope you will take time to go back through all of these Scriptures again to study, meditate upon, and let the Word take root in your heart. I pray you will be a doer of the Word and enjoy a rich new dimension in your relationship with the Lord and in your prayer life.

NOTES

[1] *Blue Letter Bible,* S.V. "Greek Lexicon : G3056 (KJV)," accessed Nov 28, 2015. http://www.blueletterbible.orghttps://www.blueletter bible.org/lang/lexicon/lexicon.cfm

[2] *Blue Letter Bible*, S.V. "Greek Lexicon :: G3618 (KJV)," accessed Jan 22, 2016. http://www.blueletterbible.orghttps://www.blueletter bible.org/lang/lexicon/lexicon.cfm

[3] David Guzik *Text Commentaries: Blue Letter Bible: 1 Corinthians.* Retrieved from http://www.blueletterbible.orghttps://www.blueletter bible.org/Comm/guzik_david/StudyGuide_1Cr/1Cr_14.cfm

[4] Ibid.

JOURNAL ENTRY

To get the most out of this chapter, take a few moments to journal your thoughts and/or prayers.

_____

_____

_____

_____

_____

_____

_____

_____

_____

_____

_____

_____

_____

_____

_____

_____

_____

_____

SESSION 4:
BEING LED BY THE HOLY SPIRIT

Ever been in a city trying to follow your Maps App—only to miss a turn or end up at the wrong destination? I don't know about you, but I am "Map App challenged" and the GPS system has to do a lot of "recalculating" when I am in the navigator's seat. Getting lost in a city can be frustrating, but getting lost in life can be detrimental.

So, what do you do when you need guidance from God? How do you know which way to go at the crossroads you face in life? How do you find God's will for your life? What if the specific answers you need for specific questions are not spelled out in black and white in the Bible? How do you know God's will on things like who to marry, what job to take, what house to buy? How do you hear from God when it comes to making decisions regarding the people, places, or things that fill your life? All of these questions can be answered with one single phrase: Be led by the Spirit! He is the best guide!

Have you ever been on a tour at an unfamiliar place, maybe a museum, a college campus, a kayaking trip, traveling to foreign nations, or moving to a new city? It's nice to have the help of a tour guide. Isn't it? They are extremely knowledgeable and well versed in everything those on a tour need to know. Not only do they have superior knowledge, they love to share their knowledge.

While the expertise of the credentialed tour guide is impressive, it pales in comparison to the expertise of the Holy Spirit—our divine tour guide through life. He has every credential we could think of and an eternal number of credentials we've never thought of. He knows everything past, present, and future. He knows everything about everyone everywhere, and with His omniscient abilities. He is most qualified to guide us. With the Holy Spirit as our Guide, we have a supernatural advantage!

Let's look at what the Bible tells us about being led by the Spirit.

A. THE HOLY SPIRIT IS OUR TOUR GUIDE THROUGH LIFE

One of the greatest benefits of the Spirit–empowered life is the ability to be led by the Spirit in the small and large decisions of daily life.

John 16:13-15 AMPC

But when He, the Spirit of Truth (the Truth-giving Spirit) comes, He will guide you into all the Truth (the whole, full Truth). For He will not speak His own message [on His own authority]; but He will tell whatever He hears [from the Father; He will give the message that has been given to Him], and He will announce and declare to you the things that are to come [that will happen in the future]. He will honor and glorify Me, because He will take of (receive, draw upon) what is Mine and will reveal (declare, disclose, transmit) it to you. Everything that the Father has is Mine. That is what I meant when I said that He [the Spirit] will take the things that are Mine and will reveal (declare, disclose, transmit) it to you.

We can learn a lot about the Godhead from this passage of Scripture. We know that the Father is seated on His throne in heaven, and Jesus is seated at His right hand. The Holy Spirit is on earth, dwelling within believers.

In your own words, explain the working relationship between Father, Son and Holy Spirit as revealed in these verses.

_____

According to verse 13, what did Jesus say the Holy Spirit would do for us? _____

According to verses 14-15, in what ways does the Holy Spirit communicate guidance to us? _____

Think of it this way, not only do we have a supernatural tour guide *with* us, we have the most advanced and supernatural GPS system living on the *inside* of us. The Holy Spirit will not only help and empower us, He will guide us each day if we will set our minds on Him and if we will listen to His guidance. When we listen to Him and obey what He leads us to do, we can live in the divine flow of the Spirit.

On the other hand, through disobedience or an inadvertent wrong turn, we can end up heading in the wrong direction. But, if we listen to the Holy Spirit, he will help us turn around and get on the right path. He is merciful and full of grace and will "recalculate" our path to help us get from where we are to where He wants us to go.

Can we pause for a moment? I believe the Holy Spirit wants to encourage many of you who feel like you are wandering around the

125

wilderness, wondering where God is. You are in desperate need of the Holy Spirit's guidance.

If you were once doing well in following the Lord but for different reasons took an exit ramp, and life has been, well, rotten-*ish*, keep reading. This is for you.

Maybe you thought the Lord was leading you to do something and you took off believing He was in it, but things didn't go so well. You prayed, believed, and kept going, but things didn't get better and the farther you went, the worse it got. Eventually, you just accepted this rough life as your new normal.

Maybe you took an exit ramp for the wrong reasons. You were offended, hurt, disappointed, or deeply discouraged, and you ran—maybe trying to get away from people, church, Christians, life or even God himself. But that hasn't turned out too good and you're tired of the constant struggle.

Maybe now is a good time to stop and assess your life by asking yourself this question, "When did you last sense the Lord's blessing, favor, peace, joy, and goodness flowing in your life?" If you can look back to a time when you were fat and sassy (I mean blessed and living the dream), God wants to help you get back to that place. It may or may not be a physical place but for sure it is a place in Him and in your heart where His love, mercy, truth and goodness flows. Just follow His guidance and obey whatever He tells you to do. Step by step, He'll renew your life!

We've all made mistakes, so no one is throwing any stones at you. Be encouraged in your desire to quit traveling on the wrong road and to leave the pattern of wandering around in the wilderness. Today, if you'll choose to turn around (aka: repent) and ask the Holy Spirit to guide you—He will! He will do some "recalculating" and as you follow

His plan, He'll lead you to the best route for getting back on the high-way of God's blessed plan for your life.

I hope this encourages you. God is for you. The Holy Spirit will guide you.

Like I said, we've all made mistakes and gone off road. I had a note taped to my mirror years ago just to remind myself, "If God seems far away, guess who moved." Perhaps you'll be encouraged by our story of completely missing the Holy Spirit's leading in a season of our lives.

I can't imagine what our lives would look like without His lead-ership. Well, actually I can. Prior to pioneering and pastoring Valley Family Church, we tried to start a different church over a year ear-lier. We were going to call it Harvest Field Church. It was a disas-ter. It lasted ten weeks. At our peak, my husband Jeff was preaching his dynamic messages to ten adults in the clubhouse of the apartment complex where we lived. Two of those members, Jeff picked up from the adult foster care home in another town, and he affectionately called them Doubt and Unbelief as they talked nothing but doubt and unbe-lief the entire time he drove them to and fro.

Meanwhile, I was the boss of kids church which included one child—our daughter, Meghan! However, I was able to double our chil-dren's ministry from just one to two in ten weeks, when little Rachel joined us. Since we met in our apartment, I also did the laundry for Melinda, one of the members of the adult service. I hated it. (Not the laundry part, the church part!) I dreaded Sundays. This wasn't a calling. This was a prison sentence, and I couldn't imagine doing this for the rest of our lives. Needless to say, we never sensed God's grace, anoint-ing, or presence. It was like sledding up a dirt hill!

So after the ten longest weeks of our lives, we told everyone, "Thanks for coming! As it turns out, we're not pastors, and this is not gonna be a church. Have a nice life." Then we cried and went into the fetal position for about 18 months trying to figure out what in the world we were supposed to do with our lives—and dying to every ambition, vision, dream, and desire we had for pastoring and changing the world. So, there you have it, "Ten Steps on How to Not Be Led by the Holy Spirit."

Eighteen months later, after the Lord had done a complete remodeling job in our hearts, He began to resurrect the idea in my husband's heart of pioneering a church. When Jeff asked me what I thought about the idea of starting another church, I rolled my eyes (always the supportive wife). However, he was serious. The Lord asked me a question one day as I was running away from the idea: "What if I am the One resurrecting this idea in Jeff?" I responded, "Please don't!" Well, you can guess who won.

We planted Valley Family Church in 1991, and if you saw our Grand Opening advertisements, not to mention our trendy hairstyles from the 90's, you could see the Holy Spirit had very little to work with. Did I mention that at the same time we were planting a church, we were producing kids like rabbits? Four kids all under the age of six! Well, thank God we had thousands of dollars stashed away to fund everything. (Uh—scratch that, we had zero dollars stashed away!) Instead, He led us to fund the ministry by using the proceeds from the sale of our one asset, a 1988 Honda Accord, and by receiving one offering a week during our Sunday services. If you only knew how miraculous that was! (Of course, if you're reading this now and feeling the warm blanket of His Presence upon you urging you to send in a hefty offering, do what you gotta do.)

So, how did we start a church with the help of three other adults and two kids, and then practically overnight (which means over the next 20 years) build a campus on 30-acres, hold multiple services in several venues and grow it to reach thousands of people each weekend—in a Michigan town with a funny name like Kalamazoo? Not with our wits, that's for sure. (Not that we didn't try to use our wits.) But, any *lasting* success we've had is the simply the result of following the guidance of the Holy Spirit.

That's how a successful life happens for all of us. When we follow the Spirit, through all the twists and turns and "recalculatings," He will lead us to lasting victory through Christ our Lord! And all the people said?

So, let's look at various ways the Holy Spirit leads us.

B. FIVE WAYS THE HOLY SPIRIT LEADS US IN OUR DAILY LIVES

1. The Spirit Leads Us by His Word

Matthew 4:4

But He answered and said, "It is written, 'Man shall not live by bread alone, but by every word that proceeds from the mouth of God.'"

What did Jesus say we are to live by? _____

_____

Can you think of examples of where the Holy Spirit led you by specific scriptures He quickened or spoke to your heart? List them. _____

_____

God's primary way of leading us is through His Word—His written Word and the words of Scripture He speaks to our hearts. Whenever we face decisions or need direction, we always go to the Word first, and we ask the Lord to give us His wisdom, answers, direction, and guidance as we read the Word. It's comforting to know that we can trust the Holy Spirit to give us His customized plan as we read God's Word and listen to His promptings.

I remember the very first time I sensed the Holy Spirit leading me from God's Word. I was a brand new Christian and really enjoying this new experience of love and inner joy and the peace of knowing Jesus was with me. Then, out of the blue, I remember thinking, "Wait, what if all of this is too good to be true?" I felt fear rear its ugly head, and I trembled at the idea the Lord was going to leave me and this love, joy, and peace was going to evaporate. That night, I practically hugged my Bible and when I started reading it, I just happened to read Hebrews 13:8, which says, "I will never leave you and I will never forsake you." When I read those words, it was as if the Holy Spirit said, "Watch this," and He peeled those words from the page in my Bible and wallpapered them into my heart. The instant flow of relief and peace this verse brought to me is hard to convey, but at once those fearful thoughts left, and it was settled. He would never leave me or forsake me. This love, joy, and peace I felt was for real and lasting!

Now over thirty years later, I can testify that I have lived by this Word from God. I have experienced some wonderful seasons of God's nearness, and I have been through some very difficult seasons that felt dry as a desert, but the Lord hasn't left me yet. At times, His presence was more known by faith than felt by goose bumps, but in every season His love, peace, and joy have been an ever-present undercurrent.

As you read the Bible, turn on your expectation and trust the Holy Spirit to quicken the Scriptures you need to live by!

2. The Spirit Leads Us by the Witness

Romans 8:5-17

For those who live according to the flesh set their minds on the things of the flesh, but those *who live* according to the Spirit, the things of the Spirit. For to be carnally minded is death, but to be spiritually minded is life and peace. Because the carnal mind is enmity against God: for it is not subject to the law of God, nor indeed can be. So then, those who are in the flesh cannot please God. But you are not in the flesh but in the Spirit, if indeed the Spirit of God dwells in you. Now if anyone does not have the Spirit of Christ, he is not His. And if Christ *is* in you, the body *is* dead because of sin, but the Spirit *is* life because of righteousness. But if the Spirit of Him who raised Jesus from the dead dwells in you, He who raised Christ from the dead will also give life to your mortal bodies through His Spirit who dwells in you. Therefore, brethren, we are debtors—not to the flesh, to live according to the flesh. For if you live according to the flesh you will die; but if by the Spirit you put to death the deeds of the body, you will live. For as many as are led by the Spirit of God, these are sons of God. For you did not receive the spirit of bondage again to fear, but you received the Spirit of adoption by whom we cry out, "Abba, Father." The Spirit Himself bears witness with our spirit that we are children of God, and if children, then heirs—heirs of God and joint heirs with Christ.

According to verse 14, who leads the sons of God? _____

_____

According to verses 5-6, what are we to set our minds upon? _____

_____

In a practical way, how do you do this in your daily life? _____

According to verse 16, what does the Spirit do with our spirit? __

The Holy Spirit witnesses with our spirit by giving us an assurance, a confidence, and a confirmation that we are God's children and on track with Him. The Spirit puts a knowing in our hearts. Someone once said, "We just know in our knower." That's about the best way to explain it. When the Spirit bears witness with our spirit, we just know in our knower, and God's Word always confirms it.

3. The Spirit Leads Us by His Still Small Voice

1 Kings 19:11-12

Then He said, "Go out, and stand on the mountain before the LORD." And behold, the LORD passed by, and a great and strong wind tore into the mountains and broke the rocks in pieces before the LORD, *but* the LORD *was* not in the wind; and after the wind an earthquake, *but* the LORD *was* not in the earthquake; and after the earthquake a fire, *but* the LORD *was* not in the fire; and after the fire a still small voice.

The Lord does not often lead us by wild, loud, spectacular signs.

What three things was the Lord not in? _____
_____

What one thing was the Lord in? _____
_____

Very often, it's the still small voice of the Spirit that leads us.

Keep in mind that sometimes the enemy tries to counterfeit the Spirit's voice by speaking to us in a "still, small voice" that breeds fear, discouragement, lack of confidence, anxiety, and frustration. This is not the voice of the Spirit. The Holy Spirit's voice will come with faith, wisdom, direction, and insight and will result in peace, power, desire, joy, and freedom.

I once worked for an orthopedic surgeon. He was a born-again, Spirit–filled man whom the Lord used to invent many of the modern day arthroscopic techniques that are commonly used today. He shared this story of being led by the Spirit. One day he noticed a rash on his hands. (Not a good thing for a surgeon!) Instead of being hasty and praying a generic prayer for His hands to be healed, he asked the Lord about it and what to do. He said inside his heart he sensed the Holy Spirit say, "Quit using the soap at the hospital." He quit using the soap at the hospital, and *viola*, his hands were "miraculously" healed!

I remember an experience I had with the Holy Spirit and His still small voice. I had just written my first book, *Getting a Grip on the Basics.* I had submitted it to a publisher twice and was rejected twice! I just knew the Lord prompted me to write that book, so although I was discouraged, I wasn't ready to quit pursuing His plan for the book. One weekend I was invited to speak at a church about five hours away, and I prayed about this book as I was driving. Here's how that prayer conversation went:

"Father, I believe You wanted me to write this Basics book. So, I now give it back to You. I ask You to get this book into the hands of all the people—pastors, Christian leaders, new and young Christians, and anyone else who can benefit from it. I pray You use it for Your glory to build up Your Church in America. In Jesus' Name. Amen!"

When I said, "Amen!" I sensed His still small voice speaking to my heart.

"Why stop with America?"

"Mmmm, well," I prayed, "Ok Father, I ask You to use this book, and help it get into the hands of anyone who could benefit from it all over the world—in every nation where they speak English. Use it for Your glory to build up Your Church. In Jesus' Name. Amen."

Again, when I said, "Amen." I sensed the Holy Spirit speaking in that still small voice.

"Why stop with English?" He asked.

"Mmmm, okay," I prayed again, "Father, I ask You to use this book all over the entire world in whatever language You want it in to help people everywhere grow in faith. Use it for Your glory and to build up Your Church. In Jesus' Name. Amen."

And, wouldn't you know, I sensed the Holy Spirit speak in that still small voice, again.

"Why stop with the earth?" He asked. (Just kidding on that one.)

Through this experience, I did sense Him enlarging my faith as His still small voice led me to pray bigger prayers.

Now over twenty years later, the Lord has surely been faithful to answer! *Getting a Grip on the Basics* has sold over 220,000 copies in English and has been translated into these languages: Mandarin Chinese, Czech, Dutch, Farsi, French, German, Hindi, Italian, Japanese, Korean, Norwegian, Russian, Spanish, Thai, Vietnamese and Waray. (And, if you are interested, you may download the translations for free from our website.) I sure am glad He spoke to me in His still small voice and helped me pray.

What about you? When you get quiet to listen to the still, small voice of the Spirit, what is He saying to you these days? _____

4. The Spirit Leads Us by His Peace

Colossians 3:15, AMPC

And let the peace (soul harmony which comes) from Christ rule (act as umpire continually) in your hearts [deciding and settling with finality all questions that arise in your minds, in that peaceful state] to which as [members of Christ's] one body you were also called [to live]. And be thankful (appreciative), [giving praise to God always].

The Holy Spirit leads us by His peace.

According to this verse, what is God's peace compared to? _____

The longer you walk with the Lord, the more accustomed you will be to flowing in His peace as the normal atmosphere of your Christian life. Sometimes we identify what the peace of God feels like by recognizing when we are not in it.

This became clear to me many years ago as a senior at Boston University. I knew the Lord had called me to the ministry, but I didn't know what that was supposed to look like. I also knew that during the last half of my senior year of college, I had a headache almost every day. I was popping Excedrin headache pills like they were candy just to get rid of the pain.

After graduation, I was planning to join the staff of Campus Crusade for Christ (called Cru these days) with whom I had been involved for several years. As I pursued the application process to go on staff, I noticed the headaches seemed to increase. I never made any connection between the headaches and the pursuit of becoming staff; I just took my Excedrin and carried on. My only other career option was to move back to my hometown and try to figure out what to do with my life.

One day, I went to visit my pastor and asked him how I could know for sure what God's will was for my life. He shared Colossians 3:15 with me and explained that I should let the peace of God be the umpire, "And let the peace (soul harmony which comes) from Christ rule (act as umpire continually) in your hearts [deciding and settling with finality all questions that arise in your minds, in that peaceful state] to which as [members of Christ's] one body you were also called [to live]."

So, I got quiet and tried to picture the peace umpire calling the shots when I thought about my two options. When I thought about going on staff with Crusade, although this made the most sense and it's what I wanted to do, I didn't feel like the "peace umpire" was giving me a green light. When I thought about moving back to my hometown, which I didn't want to do because it seemed like three giant steps backward, I felt like the umpire was flashing the green light on this option.

Even though it didn't make rational sense, I let the peace umpire rule, and I moved back home. Interestingly, although I didn't know what my future would look like, I was filled with peace and joy, and the headaches stopped immediately! I didn't take another Excedrin! So, what's the moral of the story? Follow the peace umpire! In looking back, I believe that my heart was unsettled all along. I just had not discerned it, and that's why I began to have daily headaches. It took a while for me to figure out that the headaches were a manifestation of a lack of peace.

That doesn't mean that every headache or physical ailment is the result of a lack of peace, but that experience certainly caused me to look a little more carefully at the peace meter when I have unexplained physical symptoms to see if there is any connection to decisions I have made or am pondering. (Also, at times we may have peace in our hearts, but uncertainty or doubt in our heads. Again, that's why it's always good to follow the peace in our hearts.)

On the flip side, there can be situations where someone has total peace and is walking out God's clearly laid-out plan, yet they find themselves hit with unexplained pain, challenges, and roadblocks. This may not be a lack of peace; it may simply be the enemy coming against a person to halt them in following God's plan. That's why it's best to let the peace umpire call the shots. God's peace is a safe guide. Listen to the peace umpire, and the Lord will bring you through.

5. The Spirit Leads Us by Desire

Psalm 37:4

Delight yourself also in the LORD, and He shall give you the desires of your heart.

What does God want you to do in your relationship with Him? ____

_____

What will He give you? _____

_____

Have you been delighting yourself in the Lord? _____

_____

What desires has He put in your heart? _____

_____

This is a wonderful verse with a double meaning. When we delight ourselves in the Lord by seeking Him and being content in Him, He fills our hearts with desires. Then, because we have been delighting ourselves in the Lord, He fulfills the desires He's put in our hearts!

If you've been delighting yourself in the Lord and find that you have a consistent and godly desire in your heart (like a desire to get married, have children, serve the Lord, go to college, start a business, help the elderly, and so on), you can have confidence that the Lord put those desires in your heart, and He will guide you on the route He has planned to see them fulfilled.

Let me mention one caveat. Sometimes the Lord's route isn't the shortest. While we are focused on the destination, He is interested in the process, the journey and our transformation! If it seems like it's taking a million years to get to your Promised Land, find comfort in the reality that He's working on your *life* as you journey to your *land*. Philippians tells us, "for it is God who works in you both to will and to do for *His* good pleasure," (Philippians 2:13.) There's no sense in trying to find a shortcut. In fact, it might delay the journey because when we try to skirt the Lord's plan, He has to take us on a trip to "Patienceville" where He can work with us on things like control issues, manipulation, deception, haste, impatience and other ugly traits. I know, it's a painful truth (#truthbombsidislike).

C. BEING AWARE OF THE SPIRIT'S LEADING AND HIS GIFTS

Not only does the Holy Spirit lead us in the daily affairs of life, He leads us in spiritual things and gives us the supernatural gifts of the Spirit to bless us and to make us a blessing to others.

1. 1 Corinthians 12:1

Now concerning spiritual *gifts*, brethren, I do not want you to be ignorant.

What does the Lord not want us to be ignorant of? _____
_____

That means, He wants us to be knowledgeable and aware of what? _____

2. 1 Corinthians 12:4-7

There are diversities of gifts, but the same Spirit. There are differences of ministries, but the same Lord. And there are diversities of activities, but it is the same God who works all in all. But the manifestation of the Spirit is given to each one for the profit of *all*.

Notice the same Spirit is directing the manifestation of what three things?

Diversities of _____

Differences of _____

Diversities of _____

While the gifts, ministries, and activities we have from the Lord may be different, what remains the same? _____

According to verse 7, what are the manifestations of these gifts, ministries, and activities for? _____

The Amplified Bible brings this out more fully:

1 Corinthians 12:4-7 AMP

Now there are distinctive varieties and distributions of endowments (gifts, extraordinary powers distinguishing certain Christians, due to the power of divine grace operating in their souls by the Holy Spirit) and they vary, but the [Holy] Spirit remains the same. And there are distinctive varieties of service and ministration, but it is the same Lord [Who is served]. And there are distinctive varieties of operation [of working to accomplish things], but it is the same God Who inspires and energizes them all in all. But to each one is given the manifestation of the [Holy] Spirit [the evidence, the spiritual illumination of the Spirit] for good and profit.

In other words, there are many different ways the Holy Spirit distributes His gifts and leads people in distinct operations of service and ministry, but it is the same Holy Spirit. He leads us according to whatever He deems good and profitable. It can be as simple as being led to give someone a cold cup of water or a heartfelt word of encouragement and as innovative as being led to start a ministry to the homeless in the middle of a metropolis or as unique as being led to operate a snowboarding ministry to the snow lovers of the Himalayas. The Holy Spirit is the One who is in charge of the operations, services and ministries.

Can you think of a time in your life when the Holy Spirit led you to do something good and profitable for others?_____

_____

How did He lead you? _____

What gifts, operations, service did He lead you to utilize? _____

_____

This is why it is so important that we don't judge or criticize others in the Body of Christ for the way they operate, do ministry, serve the Lord, minister in their churches, or accomplish things for the glory of God. It is not our department to judge each other's spirituality. It is our job to love and encourage one another. It is the Holy Spirit's job to lead His people as He chooses.

3. 1 Corinthians 12:3, NLT

So I want you to know that no one speaking by the Spirit of God will curse Jesus, and no one can say Jesus is Lord, except by the Holy Spirit.

Who will the Holy Spirit and His gifts always exalt? _____

_____

In other words, the Holy Spirit will never lead us or give us gifts that contradict Jesus' words or bring Him dishonor.

4. 1 Corinthians 12:7-11

But the manifestation of the Spirit is given to each one for the profit *of all*: for to one is given the word of wisdom through the Spirit, to another the word of knowledge through the same Spirit, to another faith by the same Spirit, to another gifts of healings by the same Spirit, to another the working of miracles, to another prophecy, to another discerning of spirits, to another *different* kinds of tongues, to another the interpretation of tongues. But one and the same Spirit works all these things, distributing to each one individually as He wills.

This passage describes the supernatural gifts of the Holy Spirit. What is the purpose of the manifestation of the gifts of the Spirit?____

_____

_____

These gifts are given as He wills and in order to bless and benefit others.

What nine gifts of the Spirit are listed in this passage? _____

_____

_____

The gifts of the Spirit are truly that, gifts of God's ability from the Holy Spirit. The gifts of the Spirit are demonstrations of His love and ability flowing through us to accomplish His purposes and to help others. The gifts of the Spirit are given as He wills to help and benefit people.

In pastoring and pioneering things, my husband and I have noticed that the Holy Spirit has consistently given us either the word of knowledge, the word of wisdom, or the gift of faith to minister to people and build His church. We have experienced the other gifts of the Spirit on a more limited basis as He desired and the needs required. As you reflect on your own life, you might be surprised how often He's given you one or more of the gifts of the Spirit to benefit you or help you minister to others. I hope these examples stir up your desire for all that the Holy Spirit wants to do through you.

The word of knowledge is when the Spirit gives us a small piece of the knowledge of things that have happened in the past or present. A few years ago, I was visiting with a young lady who was struggling with feelings of unworthiness and guilt. As we were talking, I suddenly knew that she'd had an abortion when she was younger and although she knew God forgave her, she could not forgive herself. This was a manifestation of the word of knowledge, not because the Lord wanted to embarrass her, but because He wanted to set her free. When I told her what the Lord had allowed me to know, she confirmed that it was true and that she had been unable to forgive herself. However, when she heard the word of knowledge, she was so encouraged to know that the Lord knew all about her and He loved her and forgave her. At that point, she was finally able to forgive herself.

The word of wisdom is when the Spirit gives us wisdom on future things. He shows us what to do and when to do it regarding a particular situation or decision. Over the years, the Lord has given me a word of wisdom when it comes to our family, ministry, and the church family we pastor. At times, the word of wisdom has come as an instruction or a knowing, as a vision or through a dream. In each case, the word of wisdom helped us know about specific things to come, what to do, and when to do it.

When our kids were in middle school and high school, the Lord gave us a word of wisdom about how to pray and parent them through that season. Neither Jeff nor I were raised in Christian homes, so we did not know what type of Christian expectations we should put on our kids when they were in middle school and high school. As a family, we raised our kids from their births with one guiding principle, "live your life to please the Lord." That was our mantra. We didn't want them to worry about being a pastor's kid or trying to live up to unrealistic expectations, we wanted them to make decisions according to what would "please the Lord." In a strange way, this took the pressure off them and helped them develop their own relationship with the Lord. When they reached the middle school and high school years, we knew they were coming into a season where at some level they would be exposed to a variety of temptations with music, friendships, parties, the opposite sex, drinking, and drugs. We'd heard too many stories about pastor's kids who rebelled in the teen years, and we really wanted God's wisdom on how parent them.

If we were too strict or over-protective, we were concerned that we would push them to rebel, or we would stunt the development of healthy coping skills. If we were too permissive, we were concerned that would put them in positions where they faced more temptations than they needed or were mature enough to handle. If we put too much pressure on them to be model PK's, we knew that would backfire. That's when the Lord spoke to my heart with what we believe was a simple word of wisdom. He said, "Your kids are not perfect. Your kids will make mistakes. My Son, Jesus Christ is the only perfect one. Pray for your children. Pray that their mistakes will be minor and that they will learn their lessons quickly." So, that's exactly what we did.

That word of wisdom helped us parent our kids. They made it through middle school and high school just fine. They weren't perfect. They made minor mistakes. We didn't freak out. They learned their lessons quickly. We survived. Today, they are young adults, and they all love the Lord. They love us. They love His church and are pursuing His purposes for them. We are so thankful for the gifts of the Spirit!

These are just two practical examples of the supernatural operation of the gifts of the Spirit and how the Lord will use them to lead, guide, confirm, and encourage us.

There is so much more to learn about these gifts of the Spirit. I encourage you to dig into the Bible and ask the Holy Spirit to show you what you need to know. He is so personal, and He knows how to give us just what we need, when we need it.

5. Hebrews 10:24-25 AMPC

And let us consider and give attentive, continuous care to watching over one another, studying how we may stir up (stimulate and incite) to love *and* helpful deeds *and* noble activities, not forsaking *or* neglecting to assemble together [as believers], as is the habit of some people, but admonishing (warning, urging, and encouraging) one another, and all the more faithfully as you see the day approaching.

As we listen to the Spirit's promptings, what are we to do for one another? _____

Can you think of a recent time when the Holy Spirit gave you a prompting to encourage someone with a word of knowledge or a word of wisdom or another gift of the Spirit? If so, describe what happened.

_____

_____

6. Hebrews 2:1-4

Therefore we must give the more earnest heed to the things we have heard, lest we drift away. For if the word spoken through angels proved steadfast, and every transgression and disobedience received a just reward, how shall we escape if we neglect so great a salvation, which at the first began to be spoken by the Lord, and was confirmed to us by those who heard *Him*, God also bearing witness both with signs and wonders, with various miracles, and gifts of the Holy Spirit, according to His own will?

How does God bear witness to His great salvation? _____

_____

_____

We can't put the Holy Spirit in a man-made box. It is the Spirit's prerogative to bear witness to the salvation Jesus purchased with His own blood by supernatural signs, miracles, and gifts. He also confirms God's Word with signs and miracles according to His will. While the gifts of the Spirit are supernatural, His signs are not mystical, esoteric, or magical. The gifts and signs of the Spirit are always congruent with the Word.

Perhaps you are seeking God's purpose for your life, and you need some encouragement. Let me share one final example of how the Holy Spirit bore witness and confirmed His calling in my life through a sign and one of the gifts of the Spirit, the word of wisdom.

145

I was a junior at Western Michigan University, majoring in biology because I thought I wanted to be a dentist. A few weeks earlier, my Bible study leader had visited me and shared Romans 10:13-15, "For 'whoever calls on the name of the LORD shall be saved.' How then shall they call on Him in whom they have not believed? And how shall they believe in Him of whom they have not heard? And how shall they hear without a preacher? And how shall they preach unless they are sent? As it is written: 'How beautiful are the feet of those who preach the gospel of peace, who bring glad tidings of good things.'" She also shared with me a booklet titled *Have You Discovered God's Plan for Your Life*. During that visit, while reading Romans 10, I felt the Lord speak to my heart with something that sounded like this: "I interrupt your life to bring you a very important message. You are not going to be a dentist. You are going to tell people about Me." This was as real to me then as it is today more than 30 years later!

Over the next few weeks, I was pondering what all of this meant when the Lord gave me a supernatural sign and word of wisdom through a short vision or daydream, if you prefer. I was the assistant director of the dorm complex, and one day while standing in my dorm room with my eyes open, I saw a room with numerous bookshelves (like a library or bookstore). In this vision, I started walking towards the shelves to see the spines of all the books. As I got closer, I could read the words on the spines. I was stunned and surprised to see my name on the spine of what looked like dozens of books. I questioned within myself, "I'm going to write books?" I wasn't even a writer! Then the vision changed and I saw a large auditorium (very similar to our current church sanctuary). I saw myself standing on the stage teaching the Bible to people. Again, I was surprised and questioned within myself, "I'm going to speak?" I was not a speaker! Then the vision ended. Writing and speaking were the last things on my list of career options at that time.

It all happened so quickly, but I never forgot what I saw. I hid that vision in my heart and didn't share it publicly for several decades. I did my best to follow the Holy Spirit and allow Him to bring it to pass. I am so glad the Holy Spirit gave me Romans 10 and that short vision because they became an anchor for my soul, along with the numerous other scriptures the Lord ministered to me over the years. The vision has been a long time coming. It didn't come to pass overnight. I have had many marvelous opportunities to quit and go to Plan B. But now over thirty years later, I can see that this gift of the Spirit was right on target.

In your own life and calling, if the Lord has given you a supernatural sign or a vision, just hide it in your heart and be faithful to follow the leading of the Lord. He will bring it to pass.

D. THE HOLY SPIRIT ALWAYS LEADS US INTO JOY AND FREEDOM

This might be my favorite thing about the Holy Spirit! He is such a joy to know and work with, and where the Spirit of the Lord is, there is freedom! Laughter, smiles, joy, and freedom are signatures of those filled and flowing with the Spirit. You might want to reread that. Being filled with the Spirit doesn't make you angry, critical, judgmental, serious or a cousin of Debbie Downer. Joy is the distinguishing mark of a Spirit-filled Christian!

The Holy Spirit makes learning and sharing God's Word a joy. The Holy Spirit makes ministering to people a joy. The Holy Spirit fills us with joy, peace, faith, and hope!

Jeremiah 15:16

Your words were found, and I ate them, and Your word was to me the joy and rejoicing of my heart; for I am called by Your name, O LORD God of hosts.

Philippians 4:1

Therefore, my beloved and longed-for brethren, my joy and crown, so stand fast in the Lord, beloved.

1 Thessalonians 2:19

For what *is* our hope, or joy, or crown of rejoicing? *Is it* not even you in the presence of our Lord Jesus Christ at His coming?

Romans 15:13

Now may the God of hope fill you with all joy and peace in believing, that you may abound in hope by the power of the Holy Spirit.

One of the core values at our church is, "Life is short. Church should be fun." Life on this earth is short compared to the eternal life we've received through Jesus, and we believe the Holy Spirit wants us to experience great joy as we flow with Him.

Let's wrap up our study of the Spirit–empowered life with the joy and freedom of the Holy Spirit!

1. Luke 4:18

The Spirit of the Lord is upon Me, because He has anointed Me to preach the gospel to *the* poor; He has sent Me to heal *the* brokenhearted, to proclaim liberty to *the* captives and recovery of sight to *the* blind, to set at liberty those who are oppressed.

When the Spirit of the Lord is leading us and upon us, what types of things will He lead us to do? _____

_____

_____

2. Romans 14:17

For the kingdom of God is not eating and drinking, but righteousness and peace and joy in the Holy Spirit.

What can you expect to experience when the Spirit is leading you? _____

_____

I love this verse because it really reveals the heart of God and the way the Holy Spirit operates. He is not the scary, intense, severe, sober, agitated, serious person some folks have made Him out to be. He is full of righteousness, peace, and joy, and He leads us into those very things every day!

3. 2 Corinthians 3:17

Now the Lord is the Spirit; and where the Spirit of the Lord is, there *is* liberty.

When the Spirit of the Lord is leading us, He reveals Jesus. What is the result? _____

_____

As we have seen in this chapter, the Holy Spirit is our tour guide through life. The primary ways He leads us is by the Word, by the inner witness in our spirit, by His still small voice, and by His peace. If and when God guides us by giving us one of the gifts of the Spirit such as the word of wisdom or the word of knowledge, it's often because we are going to need that supernatural gift as an anchor for our soul when difficult times come. The result of living in the flow of the Spirit—empowered life is freedom, peace, and joy!

4. Acts 13:52

And the disciples were filled with joy and with the Holy Spirit.

What a great scripture to finish our study of the Spirit–empowered life. This says it all!

When we are filled with joy, we are filled with _____

_____

_____

When we are filled with the Holy Spirit, we are filled with _____

_____

_____

JOURNAL ENTRY:

To get the most out of this chapter, take a few moments to journal your thoughts and/or prayers.

_____

_____

_____

_____

_____

_____

_____

_____

_____

_____

_____

CONCLUSION

Well dear friends, I hope you have enjoyed this study! I am so glad we were able to spend this time together. Can you see why I was so excited to shout "Surprise!" at the beginning?

I hope the combination of digging into the Scriptures and reading my stories has helped you see yourself living the Spirit empowered life in a fresh way. I think the best way to summarize our time together is by praying 2 Corinthians 13:14 for you,

2 Corinthians 13:14 Message
The amazing grace of the Master, Jesus Christ, the extravagant love of God, the intimate friendship of the Holy Spirit, be with all of you.

Amen.

SPECIAL THANK YOUS

They say, "Teamwork makes the dream work," and that's absolutely true about this book! While I was hunkered down on my laptop writing, these people were working wonders to help me.

Julie Werner, thank you for being the talented, insightful, helpful, patient managing editor that you are. Hard to believe we've worked together on books for over 15 years! You are such a joy to work with. Thank you for believing in the book and me!

Troy and Joyce Wormell, thank you for publishing the Word and leading Harrison House Publishers into a bright future.

Makenzie Skinner, thank you for your excellent editing expertise and making all my words legal!

Drs. Todd and Carla Stratton, thank you for being the good chiropractic doctors that you are and for being so available during my writing seasons to help my back, hips, shoulders, neck, and ribs. Your hands are anointed!

Holly Vanderroest, thank you for being a gifted massage therapist and knowing how to unkink my writing muscles.

April Wedel, thank you for the heated neck/shoulder wrap. It came on the perfect day. My shoulders and neck thank you!

Jennifer Cole, thank you for letting me use your balance ball office chair for a few days of 24/7 writing. It was a big help, and now I'm a believer!

Mary Jo Fox, Kathy Marble, Tonya Nielsen, Jennifer Palthe, Marcia Hageman, and other faithful prayer partners, thank you for your consistent prayers. Thank you for taking me on as your assignment. I have no words to adequately express my deep heartfelt appreciation. I know the Lord keeps good records of your labor of love.

Meredith Watkins, thank you for your input and editing expertise on the early draft. So appreciated.

Meghan Hock, Brodie Hock, Annie Jones, Luke Jones, Kelsey Jones, Eric Jones, Alexa Wolfe, Rhonda Rogers, and Tara Hoult, thank you for reading various chapters and giving me your honest input and suggestions. I loved hearing your perspectives! Your insights helped me greatly.

Rev. Mary Frances Varallo and Mary Jo Fox, thank you for your friendship. Your texts and words of faith, encouragement, and support came at just the right times.

Tara Danielle, thank you for being the world's best assistant and always being one step ahead. And thank you for the continual delivery of the triple shot Americanos!

Jeff Jones, thank you for being one of God's best gifts in my life and for always encouraging me in writing seasons. Thank you for picking up the slack and creating space at home and work that allows me to write with a peace-filled heart. Love you forever.

Jonesie, thank you for sitting on my lap, licking my fingers, and being our sweet Jonesie girl, the teacup poodle.

ABOUT THE AUTHOR

 BETH JONES is an author, teacher, and pastor. She and her husband, Jeff, founded and have served as the senior pastors of Valley Family Church in Kalamazoo, Michigan, since 1991. They also lead Jeff and Beth Jones Ministries, an organization dedicated to helping people *get the basics*.

Beth grew up in Lansing, Michigan, and was raised as a Catholic. At the end of her freshman year in college, she came to a personal relationship with Christ through the testimony of her roommate. It was there, at age 19, she realized God's plan for her to preach and teach the gospel through writing and speaking. She has been following that call ever since.

Beth is the author of over 20 books; including the popular *7 Basics* and the *Getting a Grip on the Basics* series, which is being used by thousands of churches in America, has been translated into over a dozen foreign languages, and is being used around the world. Beth, along with her husband and children, write *The Basics Daily Devo* a free, daily email devotional for thousands of subscribers.

The heart of Beth's message can be boiled down to a passion to help people get the basics of God's Word! Through humor, down-to-earth teaching, and practical examples, she inspires others to follow Jesus and live out the Spirit empowered faith adventure marked by God's fingerprints!

She attended Boston University in Boston, Massachusetts, and received her ministry training at Rhema Bible Training Center in Tulsa, Oklahoma.

Beth and Jeff have a growing family with two daughters, two sons, one-son-in-law, one daughter-in-law, and their tea-cup poodle, Jonesie.

To subscribe to *The Basics Daily Devo* or to see more of Beth's resources, please visit: jeffandbethjones.org or valleyfamilychurch.org

The Harrison House Vision

Proclaiming the truth and the power

Of the Gospel of Jesus Christ

With excellence;

Challenging Christians to

Live victoriously,

Grow spiritually,

Know God intimately.

PRAYER OF SALVATION

God loves you—no matter who you are, no matter what your past. God loves you so much that he gave his one and only begotten Son for you. The Bible tells us that ". . . whoever believes in him shall not perish but have eternal life" (John 3:16 NIV). Jesus laid down His life and rose again so that we could spend eternity with Him and experience His absolute best on earth. If you would like to receive Jesus into your life, say the following prayer out loud and mean it in your heart.

Heavenly Father, I come to you admitting that I am a sinner. Right now, I choose to turn away from sin, and I ask you to cleanse me of all unrighteousness. I believe that Your son, Jesus, died on the cross to take away my sins. I also believe that he rose again from the dead so that I might be forgiven of my sins and made righteous through faith in him. I call upon the name of Jesus Christ to be the Savior and Lord of my life. Jesus, I choose to follow You and ask You that You fillme with the power of the Holy Spirit. I declare that right now I am a child of God. I am free from sin and full of the righteousness of God. I am saved in Jesus' name. Amen.

If you prayed this prayer to receive Jesus Christ as your Savior for the first time, please contact us to receive a free book by writing to us.

www.harrisonhouse.com
Harrison House
PO Box 35035
Tulsa, Oklahoma 74153